AMULETS AND TALISMANS

SIMPLE TECHNIQUES FOR
CREATING MEANINGFUL JEWELRY

ROBERT DANCIK

NORTH LIGHT BOOKS

Cincinnati, Ohio
www.mycraftivity.com

13 12 11 10   5 4 3

Distributed in Canada by Fraser Direct
100 Armstrong Avenue
Georgetown, ON, Canada L7G 5S4
Tel: (905) 877-4411

Distributed in the U.K. and Europe by David & Charles
Brunel House, Newton Abbot, Devon, TQ12 4PU, England
Tel: (+44) 1626 323200, Fax: (+44) 1626 323319
E-mail: postmaster@davidandcharles.co.uk

Distributed in Australia by Capricorn Link
P.O. Box 704, S. Windsor, NSW 2756 Australia
Tel: (02) 4577-3555

Library of Congress Cataloging-in-Publication Data

Dancik, Robert.
  Amulets and talismans : simple techniques for creating meaningful jewelry / Robert Dancik. -- 1st ed.
     p. cm.
  Includes index.
  ISBN-13: 978-1-60061-161-2 (pbk. : alk. paper)
  ISBN-10: 1-60061-161-3 (pbk. : alk. paper)
  1. Jewelry making. 2. Amulets. 3. Talismans. I. Title.
  TT212.D34 2009
  745.594'2--dc22

                    2008054373

Editor: Tonia Davenport
Cover Designer: Steven Peters
Designer: Corrie Schaffeld
Production Coordinator: Greg Nock
Photographers: Christine Polomsky and Richard Deliantoni
Photostylist: Jan Nickum

DEDICATION

To my mother, without whom I wouldn't exist.
To my father, without whom my spirit wouldn't exist.
And to Robert Ebendorf, without whom this book wouldn't exist.

ACKNOWLEDGMENTS

There are many individuals I would like to thank for their advice, council, help and guidance in the writing of this book—and in a moment I shall. However, as important as these people have been, there is another "group" I feel I must thank first, even if it's only to acknowledge that without their ideas and inspiration I would have had nothing to write about at all on the subject of amulets and talismans. This "group" is the thousands of people from virtually every culture who have ever lived on the planet and who have produced amulets and talismans since before time began. They have employed an enormous and impressive combination of materials, processes and procedures to fashion an inexhaustible array of objects used for protection, evocation and remembrance. I admire these makers for their ingenuity and resourcefulness. I hope I am able to forward the ideas and concepts they established and add my thoughts to the considerable history of this subject.

As for the actual production of this book, no one has been more instrumental than my editor Tonia Davenport. She has served as sounding board, director, friend, adviser, guide and organizer extraordinaire. She has helped me run the inevitable publishing gauntlet of a first book. At the end now, I have arrived relatively unscathed. And for that—and the rest—I thank you, Tonia.

Christine Polomsky, the wonderful photographer with whom I worked on this book, is another person I must single out. I do this not just for her incredible ability with a camera but for her equally buoyant spirit and caring approach to capturing what is needed in each photo.

Outside the realm of the book world I have been blessed with lots of people who have been supportive of my writing this book; without their honest input and contributions, I would have been lost. These people include the incredibly talented and generous artists who allowed me to include images of their work: Jeannie Thomma, for all her support, especially at the beginning of this endeavor; Sherri Haab, for sharing her considerable experience as a writer and holding my hand when needed; Robert Ebendorf; Celie Fago; Tim McCreight; Jen Kahn; Susan Lenart-Kazmer; Keith Lobue; Michael de Meng; and many others for all the inspiration I didn't even have to ask for. I thank Lisa Cain, Queen of Cornwall (and elsewhere), for her spirit, help and guidance in finding so many sacred paths. I also thank my father, Milan, for having shown me that the important stuff is ours to give away, and that after we have let it all go, we still have it all to give.

CONTENTS

OBJECTS OF AMPLIFIED CONTEXT

Why do we keep items like an old ticket stub, a Grandmother's ring that will never fit, or a lock of someone's hair? Why? Because they are not just objects, they are the reservoirs of memories. They protect us from forgetting and they afford us comfort. They are symbols for people, places and events in our lives. These objects allow us access to experiences, ideas and emotions in a way that mere words or images simply cannot. Though they may not be considered valuable, we consider them highly valued.

However, ownership of these precious articles may not be enough. We often find it necessary to place these object in a different context. We may take the stone from the ring and have it reset into a pendant so we can wear it; or we place the hair into a locket; or we mount the ticket stub in a scrapbook.

This re-contextualizing allows us to invest our belief in the idea that these objects now have the power to protect, invoke or intervene in our lives with a power greater then ourselves. These are the objects we refer to as amulets and talismans.

For this book, I have designed and constructed twenty such amulets and talismans. They are all based on traditional forms, ideas, beliefs or stories. However, rather then attempt to replicate these traditional objects, the projects here are my interpretations of them. I have selected different materials, processes and procedures to make these amulets and talismans relevant to us, our world, and our time.

Each project has a set of tools, materials and instructions to help you make the project for yourself. More importantly, my hope is that you can adapt them to make them your own. I would like nothing better than to have you use all the information here and turn it to making your own meaningful objects that allow you to express yourself fully as a person, an artist and a member of our ever growing tribe.

GROUNDWORK

If you have taken a look at the table of contents of this book, you may think there is an inordinate amount of space devoted to materials, techniques and tools. Well, you're right, there is. This was a conscious decision on my part, and thankfully my editor, Tonia, agreed.

These days when making amulets, we often have two distinct considerations. What do we want to say, and how can we physically make it? Often the first aspect is already in place. "I want to make an amulet to help me with my fear of flying" or "My children have just moved to Alaska, and I would like an amulet to protect them from the severe climate." The inspiration for the amulet most often presents itself naturally.

The second part—physically making the amulet or talisman—is where we can't rely on intuition or inspiration alone to carry us through. There are technical considerations, such as how to join elements permanently and functionally, but the question of how to join elements meaningfully should be given great consideration as well.

In order to allow your full, individual artistic voice to be heard as you proceed to make your amulets, I believe it is necessary to have an understanding of as many materials, techniques and tools as possible. Why limit yourself in any aspect of the creative process simply because you can't saw a piece of metal or rivet together some bone and paper? I have included many different techniques for working with various materials so that when the time comes and you say to yourself, "a triangle of rusted metal is the perfect element to go in the middle of a dome of black Plexiglas for my amulet," you will have what you need to do just that. *Choice equals freedom.*

Many people have a tendency to shy away from techniques like sawing and forging metal or from materials like concrete because they perceive them as difficult, time consuming, expensive or needing too many tools. This is quite simply not the case. In the techniques section I have broken down the technical tasks to their rudimentary components, with detailed written and pictorial instruction. The materials section presents how to use the various materials, as well as ideas for you to ponder, regarding the symbols they can represent. Nothing you will use to make your amulets need be costly, and with the least amount of practice, your only consideration will be "What shall I make next?"

We all have preconceived notions about what makes an object beautiful, what constitutes a piece of jewelry or what sort of material is valuable. When considering your amulets and talismans, I will ask you to suspend these notions, if only for a while, and give yourself free reign to explore, experience and, yes, *play* with everything contained in these pages. Even if you don't care for a particular technique, material or tool, at least you will have garnered experience to call upon in the future, when that material or tool may be exactly what you need to fully express yourself. *Choice equals freedom.*

MATERIALS

The materials used to make the amulets and talismans in this book are many and varied. Most of them are explained in the techniques section; others are dealt with in the directions for the projects themselves.

In developing the projects, I selected materials that are durable, widely available and that require few tools and no soldering. Most importantly, I chose materials that would allow me to express specific ideas, feelings, emotions or concepts in a particular piece. Sometimes this had to do with color, sometimes shape, but often it had to do with using the references inherent in the material itself. The permanence of concrete in "The Power is Safe in the Void" (page 108) or the buttons hanging from "Closure For A Memory" (page 124) are examples of this. Keeping this in mind, I will include some possible references (historical, verbal or otherwise) associated with each material when applicable. You may want to use these references to personalize the projects or to employ them in your future work.

On these next few pages, I will introduce you to the primary materials we'll be using in this book, along with information on where to find the materials and what to look for. Following the utilitarian description of each, you'll find a short discussion on the variety of things the material itself might represent or symbolize for you in your work—possibilities to consider when selecting materials for your own projects.

FOUND OBJECTS

When I use the term found objects, I mean *any* object you may have or come by. Found objects don't have to be just happened upon one day, lying on the ground or in a trash heap somewhere. They could include a ticket stub from a movie viewed long ago

with a special friend or the hatband from a long-deceased uncle's fedora. It may well be that you find a rusty washer on the ground or a particular shell while wandering on the beach. What's important is that this object spoke to you and that you elected to keep it. I believe that indeed any object or material can be turned toward personal, artistic expression. I believe, too, that this is born out when looking at the art and artifacts of various cultures over history.

REFERENCES

The references for found objects are as varied as the objects themselves. Some objects are symbols just by virtue of what they are—a pair of dice, a watch face or a thermometer are examples of objects with references that are in the symbolic lexicon of most people (in western culture anyway). An object's reference can also be altered or changed completely by the context in which you place it. The old Monopoly piece placed in concrete and surrounded by silver may reference the keeping of a cherished childhood memory. The same piece covered with layers of cloudy epoxy resin and surrounded with rusty iron wire may indicate the loss of that memory. These objects can also be cut up and parts of them used for very specific references. Similarly objects can be combined with others to form new symbols.

METAL
The metal used in this book is in either wire or sheet form. Wire is used in a variety of ways, such as for creating jewelry findings and rivets, but can also serve as a decorative element. Metal sheet is primarily used as a substrate.

Wire comes in various sizes, colors and shapes and is available in a wide range of materials. You may be using wire made of iron, copper, brass, sterling silver and perhaps other types you find in hardware stores or in catalogs. Wire is sold in gauges using a system whereby the smaller the number of the gauge, the larger the diameter of the wire.

- Iron wire, also called black annealed or stovepipe wire, is very strong, gray to black in color and inexpensive.
- Copper wire is very pliable, easily worked with pliers, takes texture very well and can be colored with heat and patina solutions.
- Sterling silver is more expensive and has characteristics similar to copper.
- Brass is stiffer than copper or sterling and is gold in color, can be patinated with heat, takes textures well and is fairly inexpensive.

Sheet metals used for the projects in this book include copper, brass and tin; however, others such as sterling silver or thin steel may be added. You can substitute one type of sheet for another to alter the color or reference in any project. Sheet is sold in the same gauges as wire. Copper sheet in hardware and home stores is also sold as copper flashing and is denoted in pounds rather than gauges. One-pound copper is equal to 24-gauge copper. All the cutting of sheet for the projects can be done with a jeweler's saw or tin snips.

- Copper sheet is quite malleable and can be easily worked with all the tools listed or even with just your hands. Sawing copper is easy with the jeweler's saw. It can be polished, textured and forged (see page 34), and is easy to patina with heat and chemicals. If left alone, it will darken naturally. 24-gauge is the size most often used in this book.
- Brass is usually found in catalogs rather than in stores. Brass is much stiffer than copper but has many of the same characteristics when it comes to forging and cutting. Brass doesn't take a patina from liver of sulfur but can be heat patinated with great effects.
- Sterling silver is easily worked with a saw, hammers, mallets, and with most of the tools listed in the tool section. Silver is considerably more expensive and usually yields a piece with a higher perceived value.
- Tin used here is not "sheet" tin but rather tin "cannibalized" from other sources such as cans and other packaging. Cutting tin is different from cutting sheet metal, and there is a tip included for this on page 91.

REFERENCES
Metal of all sorts has a set of references steeped in history. Ages in human development are named in metal terms such as the Bronze Age and Iron Age. We talk about the golden era of an idea, fashion or belief. Our currency is metal. Your status in most areas of accomplishment is denoted as gold, silver or bronze.

FAUX BONE

Faux Bone is a new material developed for artists that is incredibly strong and easily worked with a minimum of tools. It can take on many different looks, including ivory, ceramics or wood, or it can be left as a pristine white. It is completely nontoxic and can be used both as a finished part of your amulet or as a reinforcing element for more tentative materials. It can be polished to a velvety smoothness, scratched with files to be somewhat bristly or textured to take on various patterns. It can be inlaid with many other materials and, in turn, be inlaid into many others. Faux Bone is available in sheets ranging from ⅟₁₆" (2mm) to ½" (12mm) as well as in other forms ready-made for jewelry.

REFERENCES

Because Faux Bone is a very new material, it doesn't have historical references. However, its ability to mimic other materials allows you to call upon those references by substituting the Faux Bone. This has many advantages, such as availability, cost and safety. When used in its pure white form, the material may have no reference for you, which makes it a great background for showing off other materials.

PAPER-PULP MÂCHÉ

This lightweight, extraordinarily strong material is very inexpensive and very easy to use. It can effectively imitate rock and concrete but can be shaped into virtually any form you may want. It can be drilled, filed and sawed with regular tools including the jeweler's saw. The micro-fasteners (nuts and bolts) can be placed right in the material as it hardens for very interesting cold connections. Once mixed, it can be inlayed into voids cut out in other materials, such as Faux Bone and polymer clay, and then filed and sanded to look like an inlay of rock.

REFERENCES

Paper-pulp mâché can easily be made to look like granite, concrete or other types of stone and masonry materials but with none of the physical weight. This allows an element made of paper-pulp mâché to have the visual weight of these heavier materials and therefore tap into their references. Consider an amulet you create to try to express the weight you are feeling due to an impending event. Now consider making an amulet and dangling from it, a rocklike mâché supported by a very thin wire. Can you envision how the material is furthering the idea of the piece? Hardness and permanence are other qualities conveyed by paper-pulp mâché that can be used in your work.

Standard paper-pulp mâché comes in white and gray and is water-based and nontoxic. It takes a long time to dry in the air but can be placed in an oven to hasten the process. There is a fast-set version of this material that has all the same characteristics of the standard variety but dries in minutes instead of hours.

EPOXY (RESIN AND PUTTY)

Epoxy resins (liquid) and putties are extremely versatile materials that will inlay into almost any material with ease.

Liquid resins sold under various brand names are available in hardware stores, craft stores and in some catalogs. There are also suppliers online who offer resins with particular qualities. It comes as two parts generally mixed in equal parts by volume. I heartily advise staying away from the "syringe" style of packaging, as it is a major source of frustration. The resin can be colored with paint, powdered pigments (cheap eye makeup works well), dirt, coffee grounds or just about anything you mix in. It can also be used clear to form a window or dome over inclusions in a piece. In both cases the resin is liquid enough to pour into place.

The putties, on the other hand, come with both parts to be mixed in one length of material. These should be sliced off and mixed in your hands like polymer clay. After mixing, the putty can be pushed into place for an inlay or shaped into a form for use by itself. The putty comes already pigmented in a range of grays, blacks and copperlike colors. There is also a white that can be pigmented with a little paint and generally yields a pastel tint rather than a high chroma color, but this, and any of the putty epoxies, can be painted after they have cured.

Both of these materials are mildly toxic but can be used without the need of special masks or ventilation by placing a fan at your feet that blows away from you. This is effective since the fumes are heavier than air and sink, as opposed to wafting up in your face.

Polyester resins are very different from either of these epoxies and are extremely toxic. Great care should be taken if you use these resins.

REFERENCES

Epoxy (the liquid type) is a real chameleon when it comes to possible uses and looks. It can be used to encase and protect objects and materials that may be fragile or somewhat tentative in nature. Used this way, epoxy resembles amber and can be tinted to replicate that look. Because it can also be water-clear, it can be used to give the impression that an object is under glass much the way one might display a specimen. I also use epoxy to form "windows" in materials by cutting away a space and casting resin into that space. It can be smeared out on waxed paper, allowed to dry and then peeled up and cut like a piece of clear, rigid plastic.

The putty epoxies, depending on the color infused, can be inlaid to look like the inlays you'd find on copper, ebony or wood. They can also be textured to give the appearance of shell, tar, metal or wood.

POLYMER CLAY

Polymer clay is one of the most versatile materials in use today. It behooves you to have a working knowledge of polymer clay even if it never appears (visually) in your work. It is used in this book for its ability to be squished into spaces, to take an inlay, to use as a material to inlay into other materials and as a surface onto which to transfer an image. This last use allows for an image that can be manipulated physically and not just pictorially. Polymer clay is another material that is quite inexpensive for jewelry and small objects. It is easy to use but can be taken to great heights with the right instruction. There are a great number of books on polymer clay, and I encourage you to explore this medium in more depth.

Standard polymer clay is available in several brands. They all have similar qualities, with differences in strength, plasticity, color and durability. Various brands can be mixed or used together.

Liquid polymer clay may be painted on any paper image and baked. Then rub the paper off, leaving behind just the image on the clay.

REFERENCES

Polymer clay has an almost inexhaustible ability to imitate other materials such as rock, cloth, metal, plastics and more. It can also have no real look at all, making it a very neutral material. Much like paper-pulp mâché or Faux Bone, you can use the references inherent in those materials when composing the narrative in your work. Its ability to take image transfers means you can use it like any photograph with the same level of communication of information. With the transfer, however, you can also alter it in ways you can't with a regular photo.

CONCRETE

Concrete is the general term usually applied to cement mixed with some sort of aggregate such as sand, gravel or bits of plastic, giving it greater strength and durability. Two of my favorites are patching concrete and anchoring cement. Sold in smaller quantities with or without added vinyl (I prefer without), they set faster than regular concrete, are a bit finer in texture and require no additional aggregate. Another concrete called WhimsyCrete is available online (see Resources, page 140) and is easily pigmented.

Patching concrete is available in most hardware stores. This concrete has a fine texture, is gray in color and cures in twenty-four hours. Patching concrete is good for casting, applying to an armature or filling a form.

Anchoring cement is similar to patching concrete but finer, without any aggregate and usually darker in color. It cures in about two hours and is the strongest of the cements covered here.

WhimsyCrete is available online, is white in color and comes with several small containers of very strong pigments that allow for great colors in the concrete.

REFERENCES

When you think of concrete, what characteristics do you think of? Hard, strong, impenetrable and permanent may come to mind, along with heavy, rough and cold. Think of the possibilities if you would like to express any of these concepts in your amulet. Use the material, and you harness the power of the symbol represented by that material.

MICRO-FASTENERS

The applications for micro-fasteners (nuts and bolts, threaded inserts and more) are as many and varied as the number of fasteners themselves. One important advantage for their use is that they allow a piece to be disassembled and reassembled countless times. This may be important when trying to fabricate a piece with many parts that need to be placed and then removed to allow for reshaping or refinement. Micro-fasteners also permit the use of very fragile or brittle parts that would not withstand the stress of riveting.

When used in certain ways, micro-fasteners also allow a piece to be "perched" in/on another piece so that it appears almost to be floating. If nuts are fired into a piece of metal clay or polymer clay, other elements can be bolted in place and then removed and reassembled to form a different design. Finally, the heads of the bolts, the nuts that are threaded on and the washers, may be left as is or altered to enhance the design of a piece, thus forming another layer of information and opportunity for your artistic expression.

Micro-bolts come in a few different sizes, but the ones used here are #0-80 and #2-56 and come with various type heads including hex head, slot head, Phillips head and socket head. All are available in brass or steel. Each has a specific look and possibilities for adaptation to various designs.

Micro-nuts are hexagonal in shape and made of brass or steel.

Micro-screws have the same characteristics as the micro-bolts but in a screw form.

Threaded inserts are brass "nuts" that have a wide, screw thread on the outside and a #2-56 thread on the inside to accommodate the bolts described above. These are terrific for use in polymer clay, paper-pulp mâché, Faux Bone and more.

T-nuts are similar to threaded inserts but have the addition of a broad flange at one end and no outside threads.

REFERENCES

Nuts, bolts and washers are items with a very specific set of references. No matter what the context, when we see a hex-head bolt, we associate it with something fastened and fastened securely. The same holds for screws, nuts and rivets. We have an entire set of experiences with these objects, and those experiences equate with the references they evoke. Additionally these connectors may be altered to take on other characteristics and therefore acquire different, unique references (see page 22).

GLUES AND ADHESIVES

I am not a proponent of gluing elements of a design and then relying on the glue to hold the parts together. I do however use glue to reinforce some joins and to hold parts in place while I work on them. If I use glue exclusively to assemble elements, I always give those elements a mechanical advantage as discussed in the techniques section.

Epoxy resin can be used as an adhesive. See page 12 for more information on resin.

Cyanoacrylate glue makes up a category of glue that is generally water-clear, water-thin and dries very quickly. Super Glue and Krazy Glue are common brands. The best brand I have found is Zap-A-Gap, available at craft and hobby stores and in catalogs.

PVA glue is a water-soluble glue, usually white or yellow in color, that is great for sealing images and tentative surfaces from resins and other solvents. Available in all hardware, home and craft stores.

White glue is water-soluble glue that is water sensitive after it dries. Good, all-purpose glue, but not very relievable if moisture is an issue.

PIGMENTING MATERIALS

I have combined pigmented materials into one category even though they differ from each other in most ways. Each has its own characteristics, and I encourage you to play with all of them (as well as any others you can think of) to see how each one looks in various situations. They can all be layered with the others, and this allows an infinite number of variations. When used as a final coating, wash or layer on a piece, these materials can change the entire look, feel and narrative of a piece. I have included one or two not used in the projects but that could be used when you personalize the amulets for yourself.

Shoe polish can make a piece of Faux Bone or paper go from appearing brand-new and plastic-looking to appearing one hundred years old, worn and well used. I use polish instead of cream; however, both work well. You can dissolve spices (turmeric, paprika, cayenne pepper) in neutral shoe polish to add variations of color to your work.

Acrylic paint is water soluble and available in a huge selection of colors. It may be used to pigment epoxy resin, as a watercolor wash or as an underpainting to be aged by shoe polish or other top layers of pigment.

Oil paint isn't used in this book, but it is valuable for working over a longer period of time when you don't want the paint to dry rapidly. Thinning and cleanup need turpentine or a similar solvent.

Graphite, or soft pencil lead, can be rubbed over surfaces and then gone over with brown shoe polish to make most surfaces look like bronze.

Chemical patinas are for copper, sterling silver and several other metals. Liver of sulfur is the most common and will turn copper from a very light brown to black. Green patina and several commercial patinas, such as those by Modern Options, are available in craft stores and catalogs and turn metals various colors. Follow package directions and use prescribed safety precautions with all of them.

TOOLS

Mr. Blauvelt, my seventh-grade shop teacher, was neither an artist nor one to wax poetic about . . . well, anything. He did however, bestow upon us, his eager students, several wonderful thoughts concerning the pursuits of wood- and metalworking. One tidbit of his wisdom (and one that is extremely appropriate for this section) is this: All tools are an extension of a part or function of our body. As a seventh grader, this statement made little impression on me. However, as an adult—having delved deeper into working with, buying and making tools—its importance and truth have become abundantly evident.

Many of these "body" extensions are fairly obvious: The clenched hand is a hammer, the fingers pinch like pliers, the teeth cut like scissors. However, consider other possibilities, such as the foot or knee to hold things in place while you work. Consider a screwdriver to turn a small object rather than turning it with your fingers. Or consider the teeth, this time as a reciprocating saw blade that wears through an item.

So, I thank you, Mr. Blauvelt, for such a valuable insight.

It bears keeping in mind that while this book is concerned with the making of amulets and talismans, most of these objects are in the scale and form of jewelry. Therefore, most of the tools, materials and techniques will either employ or reflect work done in a jewelry studio. This in no way means you must have a jewelry studio to make any of the projects given here. In fact, you need not have a studio at all. General-purpose tools and equipment will serve you well, and all the tools, materials and techniques covered here are readily available through local stores, catalogs and on the Internet.

The tools in this section are both hand and electric tools. It's important to note that one type is not necessarily better or worse than the other. There are times when the drill press will serve you well, and there are times when a small, handheld pin vise—rotated in your fingers—will be the perfect tool for the job. Whilst each tool has an intended purpose, many tools can be used effectively in a number of ways. I'm not trying to promote the use of pliers as a hammer, but pliers might do a great job extracting a nail if a hammer doesn't fit.

I have listed several possible tools in each section. Most of the work in this book can be done with some combination of these tools.

ANGELA BAUSUEL-CRISPIN
SPOON
Metal clay, Faux Bone

CUTTING

There are lots of tools for cutting; however, it isn't necessary for you to have them all. I will list several of the most useful cutting tools and their applications and then list some tools that may be less common but are very useful for certain tasks. You can take a look and decide which ones you will need to allow you to make what you want.

Jeweler's saw frame: (also see "Bench pin" under Miscellaneous, page 21) This can be the most useful tool for cutting most materials and objects. Though thought by some to be difficult to use, I will show you how to use a jeweler's saw easily and effectively with little effort and fabulous results. An extensive explanation of the jeweler's saw is in the techniques section.

Jeweler's saw blades: These fit the saw frame above. Some are for sawing metal, while others are for sawing nonmetallic materials.

Craft knife: (X-acto, Excel or similar) I use a knife with a #11 blade but there are many styles and sizes available.

Scissors: You'll want a pair large enough to comfortably cut thick paper and cloth.

Tin snips: These are available in home improvement stores, and a pair about 10" (25cm) in length is sufficient for most tasks.

Diagonal or end cutters: These are used to cut wire. The end cutters have a cutting edge that runs across the face of the jaws, while the diagonal runs the length. Both work well, and I suggest you try both to see which you prefer.

HOLDING

Pliers come in a huge variety of sizes and shapes, but for our purposes (working at the jewelry scale) you will need only two or three. Pliers that are about 5" or 6" (13 cm or 15cm) long are the best size. You will want them smooth-faced—meaning they have no serrations or teeth on the inside of the jaws, which can mar your work. It's also handy to have an old pair of pliers with teeth and heavy serrations in the middle for holding pipes and such. If you have only pliers with teeth, you can always put several layers of masking tape over the teeth, and they will serve you just fine.

Flat- or square-nose pliers: The cross-section of the jaws is rectangular and about ¼" (6mm) wide. Use these to make square bends and to hold coils of wire flat while making spirals and similar forms. These are the best pliers to grasp rivet wires when inserting the wire into a hole.

Round-nose pliers: The cross-section is round and tapered. Used to start spirals, bend wire into curves or loops and make "upset" textures in wires (see step 3, page 69).

Chain-nose pliers: The cross-section is round on top and flat where the jaws meet. These are used for bends, holding work while filing and general-purpose grasping.

FILING AND SHAPING

Files are usually denoted by their shape and coarseness, also known as their "cut." Unfortunately there is no standard numbering system when it comes to the cut of files. One or two files in a medium cut is all you really need to start, and you can add more as the need arises. These need not be expensive and are readily available in hardware stores and catalogs.

The two most common file types are standard files (between 6" and 10" [15cm and 25cm] long and about ½"–¾" [12mm–19mm] wide) and needle files (6" [15cm] or less in length, about ¼" [12mm] wide—generally sold in sets). Both types are good to have on hand, but needle files can't take away much material and are generally not practical for larger pieces.

Half round: Flat on one side and rounded on the other, the flat side of this file is for outside curves and straight edges, and the curved side for inside curves. The edge of this file can be used for cutting grooves and notches in the edges of your work.

Flat file: This file often has teeth on both flat sides and only one edge. The "safe" or nontooth side is for filing next to a surface that should not be touched while filing.

Round or rat-tail file: Long and tapered, this file is typically used for filing the insides of holes and for "dressing" the inside of tubing and the like.

Faux Bone shaping tool: Used to smooth and round the edges of Faux Bone on inside curves and straight sides. Can also be used on metal, wood and other plastics in the same way.

Checkering file: See Finishing, page 21.

DRILLING

DRILLS

While you can use any electric drill, it is extremely useful to have one with an "infinite" switch. That is, one that will start at 0; as the foot pedal or trigger is depressed, the drill will increase speed slowly and incrementally. Trying to drill a hole with a drill bit spinning, even at a fairly slow speed, is like shifting your car into gear and immediately going twenty miles per hour. The drill bit will "walk," and you will scratch the surface of your piece.

If you are going to invest in just one drill, I believe the flexible shaft machine is by far the best. There are lots of models available, and the drill need not be very expensive (see Resources, page 140). If you can't get a flexible shaft machine, a rotary electric tool such as a Dremel—preferably with a flexible shaft extension—is the next best thing.

Hand drill: This drill is available at home improvement or general hardware stores and works without electricity—you crank it by hand. A good amount of control is available with this modest drill.

Electric drill: This is the standard "gun-" shaped drill. They come in many sizes and types. I recommend a ⅜" (10mm) variable speed, reversing, cordless or corded.

Pin vice: This is a hand tool that holds small bits and lets you do intricate work. Try and get one with a swivel top, which makes using it more comfortable and hence more efficient.

Two-hole punch: More often available in jewelry supply stores, this small tool will make ³⁄₃₂" (2.3mm) or ¹⁄₁₆" (1.6mm) holes in metal sheet.

Flexible shaft machine (flex shaft): This great tool is good for many applications outside of drilling and typically comes with a foot pedal to control speed.

Drill bits

The drill bits used at the jewelry scale—and even a bit larger—are generally called twist bits, or sometimes fluted bits. They are made of tempered steel and can easily dull if used too fast or on material that is too hard.

When you drill, you should be able to see the waste material from the drilling coming up the length of the drill bit. If this doesn't happen, the material is either too hard, or you are not applying enough downward force on the drill. It also important not to drill too fast; generally speaking, the harder the material, the slower the drilling speed.

Unfortunately at the smaller sizes of drill bits (less that $\frac{1}{16}$" [1.6mm]), the bits are numbered rather than given a size denotation. When you order the bits, there is usually a chart to show the number of the bit, the decimal size and the metric size. Another confounding aspect is that there is no correlation between the size gauge of wire you may be using and the size of the appropriate drill bit. For instance, the drill bit for 14-gauge wire is a #52. Most projects in this book use this bit, which is equal to $\frac{1}{16}$" (1.6mm), or a #55 bit (1.3mm), which is just a hair smaller.

Hammering

Though not exotic, the hammer is still one of the most useful tools for fashioning your amulets and talismans. There are different shaped heads, faces and handles. Some are polished to a mirror finish, some are textured and some are left to acquire the scars of use and time. Hammers may also be clamped in a vise to act as a "stake" or anvil, over which you can shape or smooth metal and other materials with the use of a mallet (nonmetallic hammer). When held against a piece of metal and struck, the hammerhead may also act as a stamp.

Hammers are available in various sizes and weights. The hammers and mallets well suited for the work in this book are listed below. I also like to check flea markets and secondhand shops to find old hammers that may be pitted and corroded, as these marks on the hammer face are transferred to the material being hammered and impart a fabulous texture.

Ball peen: This has a round head on one end and flat face on the other.

Cross peen: This is curved across the face of the hammer.

Riveting: This has a flat, tapered end and a small, flat, round end.

Rawhide mallet (2" [5cm]) or dead-blow hammer/mallet (10oz): This is used when you want to change the shape of a piece of metal but don't want to apply texture or leave a mark.

Bench block: This may be an anvil, a part of a bench pin, a freestanding block or any heavy chunk of metal.

HEATING

Various projects in this book call for the use of heat. None of them require extreme or sustained heat (more than five minutes or so), and therefore there is no need for purchasing expensive equipment or making any special alterations in your work space.

Heat gun (craft): Designed for embossing powders, this tool is available at most art and crafts stores.

Heat gun (industrial): These are available at most home stores and are used to strip wallpaper. Try to get one that has adjustable temperature settings.

Toaster oven: Check for one of these at tag or garage sales. You will want to use an oven thermometer, for accuracy.

Coffee-cup heaters: These are great for gently drying small items.

Crème brulée torch: This small torch can ball up the ends of thin wires and create heat patinas on various surfaces. Available at most home and kitchen stores, it is filled with standard butane lighter fluid.

MARKING

Marking the surface of your material may be necessary to show you where to perform certain tasks such as drilling or cutting. These same tools may also be used to decorate the surface of your work or to aid in forming the material. Those listed here are standard items in most hardware stores, but additional tools can be made in your own studio. Making your own tools is not only a particularly satisfying endeavor but can yield the instrument that will allow you the exact artistic expression you desire.

Center punch: Look for a spring-loaded one, if you can. This tool makes a tiny dent on the surface and is primarily used to prepare for drilling a hole.

Nail set: This is a tapered tool used to set or countersink the heads of finishing nails, generally used by striking with a metal hammer.

Awl: Sometimes called a scratch awl, this pointed tool can pierce, make a dent or be used as a scribing tool to write or draw onto the surface by means of scratching it.

Indelible (permanent) markers: Waterproof and usually smudge proof, these are typically used in conjunction with measuring. Marks may typically be removed by wetting and rubbing with a standard pencil eraser.

Letter/embossing stamps: Sets are made of metal and are available in a number of sizes. Strike these with a hammer to imprint the indentation of a letter, number or decorative element onto the surface.

Electric engraver: One of the best tools for making controlled marks on just about any rigid material. The vibrating type is much better than the rotating type.

Punches and stamps: Punches come in a huge variety of designs and sizes. Sets may be purchased that include themed designs (southwest, water, etc.). Dapping punches are metal spheres on the ends of metal rods that are used by themselves or in conjunction with the dapping die described on page 21.

Compass and circle templates: These are both good for marking circles or parts of a circle and for finding the center of existing circles or similar shapes.

FINISHING

Traditionally, finishing a piece of jewelry is thought to be the process of taking your work and making it smooth and shiny. This method of finishing will be explained in detail in the section on surface treatments. However, this is only one way of thinking about finishing a piece and, for my money, way too limiting. I subscribe to the idea that the surface of your piece, when it conveys what you want it to, is the finish. Some of the possibilities for a finish are rough, smooth, matte, shiny, scratched, embossed, pitted, etched, carved, printed, rusty, chipped or burnished—that's just a starter list. And more than one finish may be used on a piece for terrific effect.

Here are some tools that will afford you the opportunity to impart most finishes. I encourage you to experiment on scraps of various materials, just to see what happens.

Files: My favorite is a checkering file, which has lines of tiny pyramids instead of rows of teeth. But any file may be used to create a deliberate texture on the finished surface.

Hammers: In the area of finishing, hammers are used to make forging marks and various textures on sheet metal and wire. All parts of the hammer may be used to strike a surface—not only the hammer face.

Rasps: Generally more course than files, rasps create a texture that is easily visible.

Sandpaper: Silicon carbide (for wet sanding) is my favorite, but standard garnet paper works fine as well. Sandpaper can impart a smooth or a rough texture, depending on the grade and the application.

Abrasive wheels: These are for rotary tools and include rubber wheels, grinding wheels, separating discs, brass and steel brushes, flapper wheels, burrs and bristle discs.

Burnisher: A burnisher is used to impart the shiniest surface possible on a piece of metal. Burnishers are also used to fold the edges of a bezel over a stone.

Brass/steel brushes: These metal-bristle brushes are used to polish metal.

No-scratch scouring pads: The most well known of these is Scotch-Brite. These pads can polish a surface or impart a soft matte sheen.

MISCELLANEOUS

Finally, here are a few more tools you might consider trying, as each comes with a new world of possibilities for adding elements to your work.

Triangular scraper: I use this sharp-edged tool to bevel the inside of a drilled hole and also to remove the burrs from a hole just drilled. Traditionally a triangular scraper is a tool used in printmaking.

Eyelet setter: Designed to splay the shaft of a tube or eyelet, this is typically used along with a hammer.

Dapping die: Usually used with dapping punches, this metal block with hemispheric depressions is used to make domes in material such as metal and heated Plexiglas.

Bench pin: This is used with a jeweler's saw. Made of wood, it clamps to a table and has a V notched out of it. I recommend getting one with a metal anvil attached, if possible.

Tweezers: It's nice to have both regular and cross-lock (which open when pinched together and hold when released) available for detail work or holding needs.

Bristle brushes: Buy the very inexpensive variety. I like to trim the boar bristles very short and use them to apply shoe polish as a finish because I can really work in the color with them this way.

TECHNIQUES YOU'LL WANT TO KNOW

The methods presented here represent a number of ways to physically hold elements together. However, that is not their only function. I believe that whenever possible, the way elements are held together should forward the idea of what you want to say in the piece. Each connection will have a reference, and those references become part of the narrative of the piece. We associate nuts and bolts with things that are assembled; rivets usually imply strength; and tube rivets not only imply strength but allow you to see through the piece at the same time.

Surface textures and treatments, too, have references and will allow you to add not only interesting visual effects but also to add to the narrative of the piece. A dark patina that is worn off may speak to the age of an object, while scratches may symbolize that someone handled the object or that it was subjected to a certain type of use.

WIRE WORK

The wire used for creating eyes, loops and jump rings ranges from 14-gauge to 22-gauge in this book.

WIRE COILS

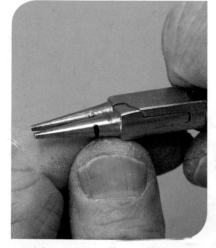

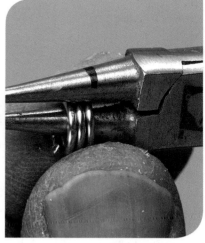

1. Make a mark on your pliers with a permanent marker at the spot that will form the size coil you want. Insert the wire between the jaws at the mark and grasp the wire lightly with the pliers.

2. With the wire hanging down, push the wire around the bottom jaw with the thumb of your other hand while you twist the pliers away from you.

3. Keep pushing and twisting while feeding the wire in the side of the loop near the handle. The coil will start to form on the other side of the loop (toward the pointed end). Keep coiling until you have the length of coil needed.

A wonderful jeweler from North Carolina, Marlene True, gave me this jump-ring jig, and I have found it one of the handiest tools I own.

JUMP RINGS

1. Start with about 4" (10cm) of a two-by-four and cut a V notch from the top about 1½" (4cm) wide at the top and 1½" (4cm) deep. Attach a piece of clear acrylic sheet to the front with two screws and saw a slot straight from the center top of the V to the bottom of the V. It's helpful to have about 1" (3cm) of wood not covered by the sheet so you can clamp the jig in a vise.

2. Thread a wire coil (see page 22) onto the blade of a jeweler's saw. (See page 30 for instruction on disengaging the blade of a saw.)

3. Slide the saw blade down the slot in the acrylic sheet so the coil rests in the V of the block and is pushed against the back of the sheet. Tilt the saw down slightly and saw through the coil, yielding individual jump rings.

4. Alternatively if you don't have a jig, you can hold the coil by hand and saw from the inside of the coil out.

EYE PINS

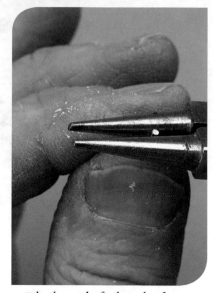

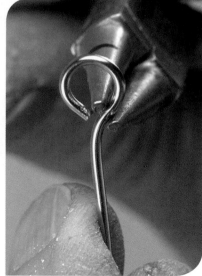

1. File the end of a length of wire to remove any burrs and to square it off. Using round-nose pliers, grip the wire at the very end.

2. Make a complete loop at one end.

3. Bend the wire back at the connection of the loop to center the loop over the length of the wire.

POINTED WIRE

1. Make a tapered groove in your bench pin using the edge of a half-round file.

2. Place the wire into the groove and file the wire with the flat side of a file, turning the wire slightly after each pass.

3. Continue filing until you get the desired point.

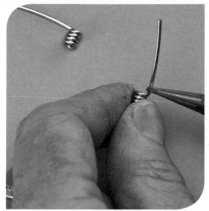

1. Mark your round-nose pliers at the same diameter as the thickness of your cord and make a coil of at least four wraps, leaving about 1" (3cm) of wire tail at the end of the wrap. Using the point of your round-nose pliers, grasp the tail where it leaves the coil and bend it up to be in line with the coil. Create two of these.

2. Beginning with one coil for the latch, grasp the wire about 3/8" (10mm) from the end with the midpoint of the round-nose pliers and form a U so the end winds up touching the coil.

3. For the hook, use the other coil and hammer the last 1/8" (3mm) of the wire tail flat.

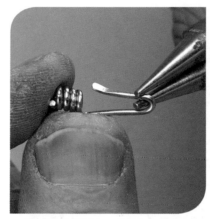

4. Create a tiny crook on the flattened end using round-nose pliers.

5. At about 1/4" (6mm) from the loop, bend the wire back toward the coil to create a U-shaped hook.

6. Slide one coil onto the end of the cord and crimp the end of the coil a bit with pliers.

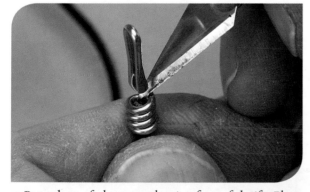

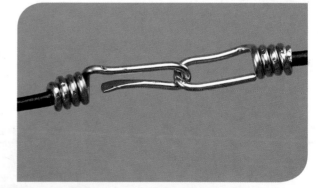

7. Put a drop of glue onto the tip of a craft knife. Place the knife tip to the end of the coil and let the glue wick into the cording.

8. Repeat for the other coil. Together the two work as a closure for cord, rubber cord, snake chain or leather thong.

RIVETS

Wire, nail and blind rivets are all used throughout this book, and each has its own characteristics and references. One requirement of all these rivets is that the hole into which the rivet is placed is the exact size of the rivet material used. It's not difficult to do, just make sure the drill bit you use is the same size as the rivet material. The size for both is given in each project. In order to keep the rivet from flattening when the second end is hammered, place the material on a thin piece of leather. For the demo images here, I'm using large-scale models, along with the actual materials, to make it easier to see.

BASIC WIRE RIVET

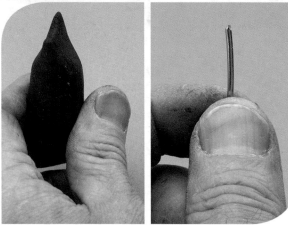

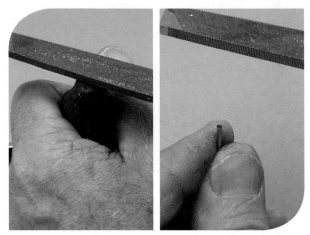

1. Begin by cutting a piece of wire about 1" (3cm) long (this will allow for easy handling). Drill the hole for the rivet the same size as the wire you selected. Note that no matter what type of cutter you use, you will have a bevel at the end of the wire.

2. The bevel needs to be filed off so the end of the wire is flat and perpendicular to the length of the wire. It's also important to remove the tiny burr that forms from filing the end of the wire. The best way to do this is to gently pull the file backward around the tip of the wire, taking care not to round over the end.

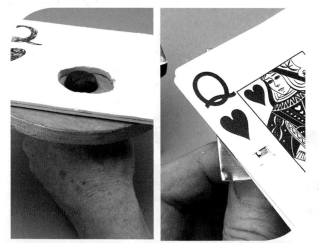

3. Insert the wire into the hole by grasping it about ½" (12mm) down from the tip with flat, smooth-faced jaw pliers and twisting it up through the hole. Take care not to rock it back and forth, or this will widen the hole. The wire should protrude from the hole about the thickness of two playing cards (make yourself two stacks of two playing cards taped together and punch a hole through each stack).

4. To trim the other end of the wire, turn the piece upside down, with the cards on the bottom and the wire through the holes in the cards. With the metal faceup, put two more cards, with a hole punched through them, over the wire and trim the wire flush with the cards.

5. File the point off this end as well. You can leave the cards in place to protect the surrounding area and file right down to the surface of the cards.

6. Using a round-faced hammer, tap around the edge of the wire to form the rivet head into a mushroom-shaped dome. Turn over the piece and form the head on the other side in the same way. A flat hammer will form a flat head that is very sharp at its edges and will catch and potentially tear anything it rubs against, so using a round-faced hammer really is preferable.

BLIND RIVET

There are two reasons this is called a blind rivet. One reason is that if you use the same metal for the background and the rivet, the rivet can't be seen. The other reason is that the rivet is entirely flush with the surface, so it can't be felt either. Even if not used for holding, this is a great way to have smooth metal dots as surface decoration in your work. It's important to remember that the surface needs to be filed and sanded after the rivet is set, so this rivet is not for a finished surface.

1. Begin as in step 1 on page 26. Before you insert the wire into the hole, form a bevel on one or both sides of the hole by placing a triangular scraper into the hole and twisting it around several times (alternately, a drill bit slightly larger than the hole size may be used to form the bevel, but make sure to do it by hand and not with an electric drill).

2. Hammer the rivet as in step 6 above so it spreads and fills the bevel around the hole. File the dome of the rivet flush with the surface of the metal.

TUBE RIVET

1. Determining the length of the tubing is just like trimming a piece of wire for a rivet. Use the process of two playing cards on either end of your surface and mark where the tubing will be cut using a permanent marker or scribe.

2. Make a slot in your bench pin with the saw and start cutting the tubing with the saw already in the slot.

3. To file off any burrs on the tubing, hold the tubing with round-nose pliers, but don't squeeze too hard, or you will dent the edge of the tubing.

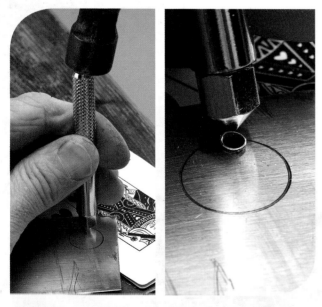

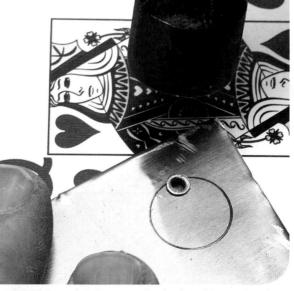

4. With the tubing inserted into the hole, support the metal from beneath by putting the tubing through the hole in two playing cards on the bench block and splay the tubing with an eyelet setter or flaring tool. Repeat for the other side (no cards necessary).

5. After the tubing is completely flared open, finish the flange you created by tapping gently with a hammer. You can also impart texture to the flange with different hammerheads, stamps and chisels.

MICRO-FASTENERS

The attachment methods we've explored thus far have been connectors we would fashion ourselves. However, this need not always be the case. The next time you're in a hardware store, take a look around and you will see that there are literally hundreds of mechanical connectors available. In addition to standard nuts and bolts, there are lots of variations easily adapted for use in your amulets.

The instructions for nuts and bolts are quite straightforward, and, while I list two methods and a variation here, there are countless combinations and variations possible. My advice is to get some nuts and bolts and play. (For more on micro-fasteners, see page 14 and also Resources on page 140.)

1. There are many different types, sizes and colors of micro-fasteners available. Consider the heads of bolts for reference in your work. What we call a Phillips head can also be thought of as a round dome of metal with a cross or X indentation. Now consider filling that cross with colored epoxy or polymer clay. It is no longer a bolt head but a silver dome of metal with a colored cross in the center—a design element just fraught with possibilities!

2. You can even alter the appearance of nuts by carving into them with a needle file. One result of this is that of a sort of petal appearance.

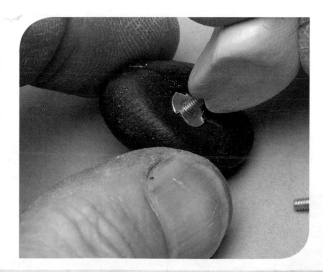

3. When you want to add a T-nut or a threaded insert into your material, like polymer clay or concrete, screw your screw into the insert or nut and then imbed it into the material. (Remove the screw before baking or curing.)

SAWING

A jeweler's saw is an inexpensive and easy-to-use tool that can cut everything from the most delicate paper to ¼" (6mm) steel with more accuracy and detail than just about any other hand tool. I recommend a frame that is either 3" or 4" (8cm or 10cm), which is the distance from the metal frame to the saw blade. The jeweler's saw is used with a bench pin. Bench pins come in different styles but all function in the same basic way.

I really encourage you to get comfortable with the jeweler's saw. Whether you want to have the tiniest stars cut out of a piece of sheet copper, lines as thin as hairs cut through baked polymer clay, letters cut into Faux Bone for epoxy inlay or spiral shapes cut into a piece of sterling silver, the jeweler's saw is the only tool that will perform all these tasks. Note: The techniques are the same for right-handed and left-handed users alike.

INSTALLING OR CHANGING THE BLADE

1. This set of instructions is a bit lengthy. However, if you go step by step, it will lead you to success with your saw and ultimately cut down on frustration. Not all the instructions are pictured here.

Position yourself about 12" (31cm) from your worktable (your table will need to be between ¾"and 1¾" [19mm and 4cm] thick). Grasp the saw-frame handle with your right hand, with the rest of the saw frame below the level of the handle. You will notice a small piece of metal protruding from the frame opposite the handle (the tail end). Rest that piece of metal on the edge of the table and lean into the saw handle with your stomach so the saw is held between you and the table and you have both hands free.

Take one of the saw blades and look at it from the side. You will see that there is a series of teeth leaning one way or the other—I will call this pointing. Hold the blade in your left hand so the teeth are facing upward and pointing toward the handle. With your right hand, open the thumbscrews at both the handle and tail about a half turn.

Insert one end of the blade into the space between the rectangular piece of metal next to the tail-end thumbscrew and the saw frame. Tighten the tail-end thumbscrew with your right hand.

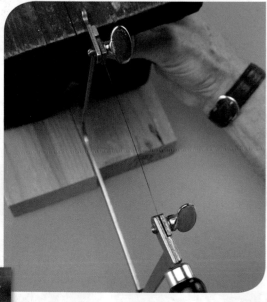

2. Check to see that the handle end of the blade is in line to go into the corresponding slot between the handle-end thumbscrew and the frame. If not, loosen the tail-end thumbscrew and adjust the blade. Check, too, to see that the end of the blade is about halfway into the slot. If not, loosen the thumbscrew at the bottom of the saw frame, adjust the frame accordingly and tighten the thumbscrew.

Take the handle in your left hand, and with the tail end still hooked onto the table edge, push the saw frame into the table. You will see the saw frame bend and the blade go into the slot at the handle end. While holding the frame bent, tighten the handle-end thumbscrew to hold the blade. Slowly let the frame out and feel the blade. It should be very taut and ping when plucked with your fingernail.

1. Begin by hammering your metal flat from both sides with a rawhide mallet or dead-blow mallet.

2. Draw or scribe your shape to be sawed on the metal. Position your workpiece so the section you're sawing is located over the V cutout. Grasp the handle of the saw as you would the handlebar of a bicycle. Let your thumb go around the handle and overlap your forefinger rather than lining up your thumb with the handle. With your other hand, hold the work by placing your fingers on top and your thumb below the bench pin. Let your elbow relax to your side; lower your shoulders and breathe—really, breathe.

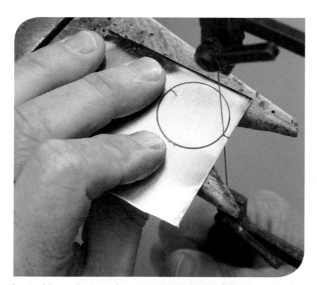

3. Holding the saw frame so the handle is vertical, bring the tail end of the blade to the edge of the workpiece between the fingers of the V slot. Tilt the handle back towards you slightly and rotate it slightly to the right (if you're right handed and left if you're a lefty). Push the saw upwards to wear a bit of a groove in the edge of your workpiece.

Remove the saw and reposition it so you can repeat the previous motion. When you have a good groove in the side of the piece, start sawing slowly and gently up and down. As you do this, begin to straighten the saw so the handle is vertical and you are sawing straight away from yourself. Don't push the saw forward; let the saw do the work.

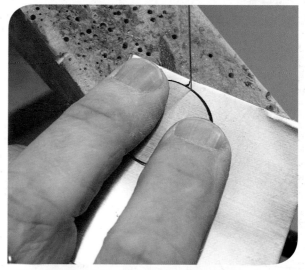

4. When you need to turn the blade, keep the saw moving up and down the entire time you are trying to turn. While moving it up and down, rotate the saw frame slowly to bring the blade in line with the new direction, or it will become stuck. If this happens, loosen your grip on the workpiece, shake it a bit with the saw, grasp it again and continue sawing.

1. I call this the "knee trick." I know this sounds odd, but it really works. If the saw gets stuck while sawing, lift your right knee up so that your knee touches your right hand (lefties, left knee). While pressing up with your knee, pull down on the saw; the position of your knee will stop you from suddenly snapping the saw downward when it dislodges from the metal, which usually results in the blade breaking.

2. Another common problem when you're sawing is that the metal keeps bobbing up and down with each saw stroke. To avoid this, position the forefinger of your holding hand behind the blade as you saw. This will stop the piece from flopping up and down and make the difference between easy sawing and more difficult sawing.

PIERCING A WINDOW

Piercing refers to cutting pieces from the inside of a sheet of material. Think of making a doughnut form from a sheet of metal. You could cut the outside circle easily enough, but to get the inside circle out you would need to pierce the piece. This method of sawing can yield cutouts that may be left as negative spaces or filled with various other materials for inlays (see page 79). Sometimes you pierce for the shape from the inside as opposed to the space left behind. Perhaps you have an old tin can with an interesting image printed on the side. You want to retain the can but cut out the image (see project 90). This is where piercing comes in.

1. Draw the shape that you want to pierce on your material. If the space is what you want, mark just inside the shape. If the shape is what you want to cut out to use later, mark just outside the shape. The example above is for the negative shape. Use a center punch to form a small divot for the drill so it won't "walk" (slip) when you start drilling.

2. Drill the hole as close to the line as possible. A $1/16$" (2mm) (#52) drill bit is used here, but any small bit will do.

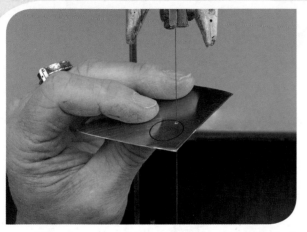

3. Holding the saw in place on the edge of the table with your stomach—so you can use both hands—thread the blade through the hole in the material. Hold the saw handle with your left hand, flex the frame as before, insert the blade in the handle end and tighten it. It is important to position the drawn shape toward the tail end of the frame.

4. Place the material, drawing side up, on the bench pin and saw as usual.

FAUX BONE AND PLEXIGLAS

Faux Bone is an incredibly useful material used in several projects in this book. It can be filed, hammered, polished, drilled, stamped, inlayed, dyed and painted. You can heat and bend it with nothing more than a small embossing heat gun. Faux Bone is so strong you can rivet on it, die a form right into it or hammer metal around it. When finished, it can look like ivory, have the patina of aged ceramic or be polished to a pure white. It is completely nontoxic, so it can be used without any ventilation problems.

Plexiglas is another wonderful material with enormous potential and vast possibilities. If you look at the project on page 130, you will see that Plexiglas has been turned into a hollow bead, thus combining the traditional form of a bead, the processes of a modern material and the inclusion of very personal items.

The technique pictured here is for sawing, which is done with a traditional jeweler's saw outfitted with a special blade. These blades still allow the incredible detail you can achieve with this saw, but with a blade that almost never breaks—really, they will not break under normal use. Alas, these special blades are not for metal but can easily cut most every other material you may use.

1. Pictured is ¼" (6mm) Faux Bone being sawed with the special nonmetal blades mentioned earlier. All techniques are the same as when you saw metal, except that the blades don't bind as with normal blades in plastics, and you can safely back the blade out of the material without fear of breaking the blade.

FILING, SANDING AND POLISHING

Many of the raw materials we use—metal, Faux Bone, paper mâché, etc.—need to be smoothed, shaped and formed after being cut to size. Even when cut with a shear or tin snips, metal has sharp edges that need to be "dressed" or smoothed before it can be handled or worn without fear of cutting or scratching. You may want to leave certain marks as evidence of the processes the material has gone through. Or you may want to smooth a material completely so that you can put back into the material only those marks you choose. Much like using certain connections to assemble the elements of your pieces, the marks you leave help you to forward the narrative of your amulet.

After all the sanding is done, you can use various waxes and other coatings on the work. Shoe polish is my favorite. Tinted shoe polish can add a bit of age to new materials and impart a lovely soft finish. If you have a buffing machine, you can also buff your work with a clean, muslin buff with no compound on it.

FILING

1. Select a file appropriate to the shape you are filing. If you have an inside or concave curve, the round side of a half-round file is best. For flat sides and outside curves, the flat side of a file is preferable. Always utilize the largest file you can comfortably use on a piece. To file, hold the work so the edge to be filed is up and pointing away from you. Make an X (not a "cross") between the file and the work. Start at the tip of the file and the end of the work closest to you.

2. Push the file along the work as well as along the length of the file. You can use a sort of grazing action rather than digging the file into the work. To round the edge over as in this image, tilt the work a bit with each file stroke to start removing material from the flat side. You should wind up with a series of flat "facets" from the file, which will be removed in the sanding process.

SANDING AND POLISHING

All sanding in this book is done with silicon carbide (Wet & Dry) sandpaper and lots of water, unless otherwise stated.

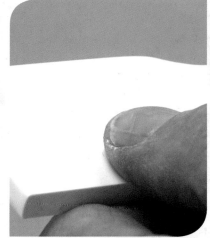

1. After filing your piece to the form you want, begin wet sanding with #320-grit sandpaper. This grit will remove the facets left by the file and yield a smooth, matte finish (possibly the final finish you want). It's best to cut your sandpaper and leave it sitting in a bowl of water to keep it supple and to let the particles that stick to the paper during the sanding process slough off into the water.

2. Continue wet sanding, progressing to #400-grit and ending with the #600-grit. After the piece is as smooth as the #600 paper will get it, you can impart a wonderful sheen by turning over the #600 paper and rubbing vigorously with the back of the sandpaper.

3. If you would like an even higher polish, rub your piece on the palm of your hand and then rub it quickly and vigorously on the leg of your pants. (I know it sounds odd, but it really works—Levi's jeans work best.)

Remember that shiny and smooth is not the "correct" finish, but is just one of many finishes you will achieve along the way. You can also have different finishes on different parts of the same piece.

BELT SANDER

When using the belt sander, it's important to keep in mind that the sander removes material much faster than any other method of finishing discussed here. Therefore proceed slowly and gently and always keep the work moving, or you will sand deep grooves into your work. The sander is usually used to change the shape and form of material rather than as a surface-finishing tool. But, if used gingerly, the sander can put very interesting lines and patterns on the edges and surfaces of a piece.

POLYMER CLAY

Polymer clay is another of those materials that can be used in a myriad of ways. It can imitate other surfaces and materials (stone, wood, ivory), hold objects in place, be polished to a high sheen, be textured or stamped. It can be inlayed into various materials and can itself be inlayed (see Rune Necklace, page 68). It is malleable, so it can be forced in and around objects or rolled into thin sheets. The colors may be mixed with results similar to mixing paint, and different colors may be combined in the same piece to form complex patterns. There are numerous books on the use of polymer clay, and you can check the references for my recommendations.

CONDITIONING

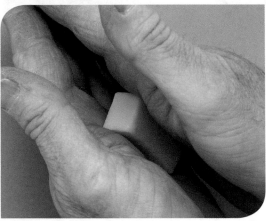

1. Cut off a segment of clay and begin to soften and work it in your hands. If pieces crumble off, just press the wad of clay into them to pick them up and continue.

2. Roll the piece into a coil between your hands. Avoid the temptation to roll the clay on the table, as this will serve only to cool the clay.

3. Fold the coil in half, twist it and roll it into a coil again. Repeat this for about five minutes until there are no more cracks when the clay is folded and pulled apart quickly. Alternately you can roll the clay through a pasta machine set to the widest setting about twenty-five times.

1. Form or roll out the clay into the shape/form you want. Make indentations in the clay, using stamps, a craft knife, carving tools, the edge of shaped pieces of metal—anything that will yield an indentation at least $1/16$" (2mm) deep.

2. Bake the clay according to manufacturer's instructions. Condition a small amount of a contrasting color of clay and press/smear it into the indentations of the baked piece. Bake the piece again.

3. Use a medium file to remove the portion of the second color that is solid. This will reveal the inlaid portion that is beneath.

4. Sand and polish and you're done. (See Sanding and Polishing, page 35.)

CONCRETE

Concrete may not be the most obvious material for jewelry and personal adornment. However, concrete brings with it many references that can be used effectively when fashioning your amulets. It speaks to permanence, longevity, hardness, building and assuredness. So if you want to include any of these concepts in your amulet, using concrete is a quick way to express it. Technically concrete is actually cement mixed with some sort of aggregate consisting of sand, gravel or other small particles. Some of the "concrete" used here is anchoring cement, which tends to set and cure faster and is a bit less porous.

1. Polymer clay makes a good mold for casting concrete forms. You can place objects in the bottom of the mold; when released, the objects will be caught in the concrete. You can also cast into any plastic container, into sand or into ceramic clay.

Another option is to prepare a bezel or box from sheet metal (see page 135) and then fill the box with concrete. In this case, the concrete remains permanently in the form.

2. To begin, spoon some concrete into a clear plastic cup (the clear plastic lets you see if there are dry places while mixing). Add a spoonful or two of clean water—but err on the side of too little.

3. Use a craft stick or palette knife and begin mixing. The mixture should be dry and very crumbly at this point.

4. Continue adding very small amounts of water until the mixture is smooth and looks wet on top but isn't actually runny.

3. Fill your vessel or mold and tamp out the air by bouncing it in your hand or pounding on the table it's sitting on.

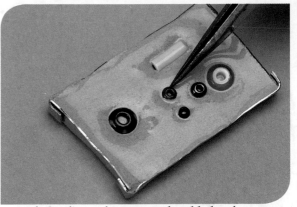

4. Beads or other inclusions may be added to the concrete while it is still wet. I prefer to use tweezers to add small things. Set aside to cure.

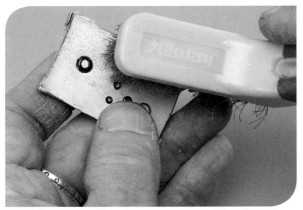

5. Scrub the cured bezel piece with a stiff brush to clean excess concrete from the beads and to reveal the inner characteristics of the concrete.

6. When the concrete has cured in the mold, it will easily pop out of the mold.

PAPER-PULP MÂCHÉ

When I introduce paper-pulp mâché in my workshops, people envision strips of newspaper dipped in wheat paste and placed over balloons; they usually look at me like I am nuts. Paper-pulp mâché, as referred to here, is shredded paper pulp combined with some sort of cementious material, most commonly a type of plaster. Once hardened, the mâché can be treated much like a piece of wood; it can be sanded, sawed, filed, drilled, textured, polished, collaged upon, leafed, patinated or covered with any surface coating you choose.

Lots of "stuff," in addition to pigment, can be mixed into the pulp: Fibers, other papers, concrete, plaster and plastic are examples. If you mix in stuff that can be filed and sanded, they will appear on the surface, suspended in the mâché for a terrific effect. For yet another effect, epoxy can be dribbled into cracks and crevices, allowed to harden, and then filed, sanded and polished along with the whole piece so that the piece begins to resemble stone with veins running through it. You can use polymer clay the same way—that is, forcing conditioned clay into cracks or areas that have been cut or drilled into the hardened mâché and then baking it to harden the clay.

I have also found paper-pulp mâché invaluable for reinforcing very thin and tentative materials. This allows me to employ the more vulnerable material in places where structural integrity is needed. There are several brands of paper-pulp mâché, and the one I am using here is Celluclay. I have found it the most reliable and the easiest to find in stores and online.

1. Put a small amount of Celluclay into a plastic zippered bag and break it up evenly with your fingers. Pour in a bit of water (see package instructions), and with the bag sealed, knead it together. Add more water as needed, but it's better to keep things on the dry side rather than add too much water. Ideally let the bag sit—airtight—overnight, but this isn't mandatory.

2. When your mixture is the consistency of bread dough, that's enough water. At this point you need to remove it from the bag and start breaking it up to see where the dry spots are inside the mixture. Keeping your hands wet during this process will stop the mâché from sticking to your hands and also add the little moisture needed to finish wetting the dry areas.

3. To make the mâché look like rock, add some acrylic paint directly onto the mixture.

4. Start breaking the mixture apart and recombining it to distribute the pigment throughout. Keep doing this for several minutes. The mixture will appear to be completely one color because it gets covered with paint from your hands. However, when dried and filed to expose the mâché just below the surface, you will see it is still mostly white with veins of color running through.

5. When the mixture is as you want it, shape it into whatever object/shape you desire. Set aside to dry (see package instructions).

6. When your paper-pulp mâché form is dry, it can be filed to remove the paint "skin" to reveal the vein pattern you created by mixing in the pigment. The piece can also be sawed with the nonmetal blades and treated in any of the ways outlined earlier.

SURFACE TEXTURES

The surface of an object contains a world of information. Origin, age and how the object has been used may all discerned just by observing the surface. The counterpoint to this is the object whose surface belies its beginnings and masks the intentions of its maker. Both speak to us, and both have their place when you make amulets and talismans. While you are forming your materials, you have the capability to infuse your pieces with whatever sort of "history" you choose. If you think of the elements of an amulet as the characters in the story you're telling, the surface of each element is like character development. Scratches may indicate where it came from; dents can indicate hard times it has gone through; cracks could be traumas; and polished areas could be positive events or successes. I encourage you to come up with your own set of surface symbols.

The instructions here address how to put a few different textures on just two types of material for your work. However, these techniques are applicable to all rigid materials. Obviously there are an infinite number of possibilities, so I suggest you start with these and expand them as you get further into your work. You may even want to create a catalog of textures on different materials so you can choose as you go along in any particular piece.

FAUX BONE

Faux Bone is a terrific material on which to put texture. After sanding to a smooth finish (see Sanding and Polishing page 35), you can add scratches with coarse sandpaper, rotary tools, an awl or, as in this case, a checkering file.

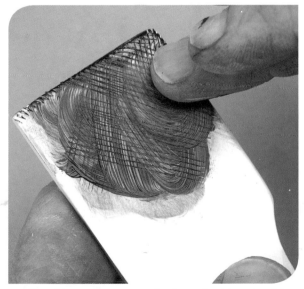 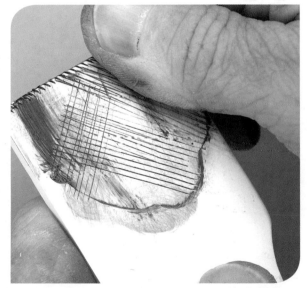

1. After the surface is scratched, sand with some #600-grit sandpaper to remove the burrs left by the tools (these may also be left as is). Rub acrylic paint over the surface, making sure it gets worked into the grooves, scratches and other marks you have made.

2. Begin to rub off the paint and you will see that the paint remains in the scratches. You can remove more of the paint with a damp cloth or fine sandpaper; this also allows you to be very selective as to where the paint remains. More, different colors of paint can be added in the same places or in different sections of the same piece. As with polishing, after the paint has dried I usually do a light sanding with #600 sandpaper, rub the piece in my hand and then rub it on the leg of my pants.

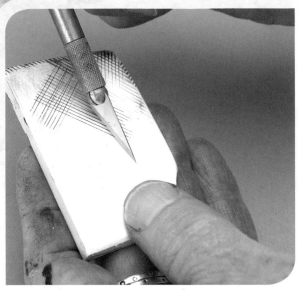

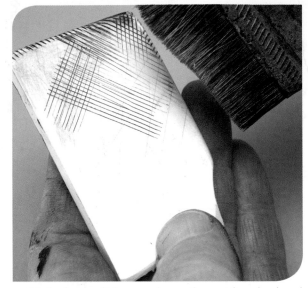

3. To add some aging, begin with a brand-new craft blade and swipe it over the surface several times in a random fashion (or deliberate if you wish).

4. Work shoe polish over the surface with a dry brush that has been trimmed short. Rub away as much or as little of the shoe polish as you like.

HAMMERING

The use of hammers is as old as humans. The shape of a hammer even comes from the shape of our arms and hands. There are hundreds of shapes of hammers, and each has its own mark or "signature" when struck on a piece of metal. I am illustrating just two hammers here but will discuss how to make your own textured hammer on the following page. For the hammer to leave marks, the metal must be hammered on a metal surface such as an anvil or bench block.

1. The ball-peen end (face) of a hammer (*peen* means "curved") creates small round dents in the surface of the metal.

2. This hammer face is called a cross peen (curved across the face of the hammer) and creates line-shaped dents. (Or crosshatched dents, if the metal is turned ninety degrees and hammered again.) If the corner of the face is used, it makes small triangular-shaped dents.

3. The same hammer may have different-shaped heads at each end. The other end of the cross-peen hammer is a broad, slightly curved face and makes larger round dents for yet a different texture. The texture at the edge is made by hammering with the cross-peen face on the flat edge of the metal.

CHECKERING FILES

Checkering files are my favorite tools for putting texture on just about any surface. They aren't used for smoothing or forming but solely for imparting texture. Checkering files come in several different coarsenesses and can be used in a number of ways. These files are a bit expensive but are well worth the cost. They are also the type of tool you buy only once in a lifetime—I've had mine for twenty-five years. (See Resources on page 140.)

1. Checkering files create parallel lines when pushed or dragged across a surface. When crisscrossed, they form a crosshatched or checkerboard pattern.

2. Checkered files can also be used to form a serrated edge on metal and other materials.

TEXTURED HAMMER

In addition to using an existing hammer to texture a surface, you can turn just about any hammer into a textured hammer by "carving" into the face. When this is done, every time you strike the metal with the hammer, the metal takes on the texture of the hammer—only, in reverse. This means if there is a groove in the hammer, it registers as a raised line in the metal.

Any hammer can be textured. You can start with a fairly new hammer and put in all the marks you want, or you can use a hammer with dents or dings already. Either way, you can change the face as you go along for other interesting textural effects.

1. Clamp the hammer in a vise with the face up. Lines can be added with the edge of a file or with a separating disc or similar accessory in a rotary tool such as a flex shaft or Dremel.

2. Dents can be added by hammering the face with a center punch, and random marks can be added with the corner of a chisel or various burrs and grinding stones in a rotary device.

3. The surrounding area can be polished with wet sanding or left with the background texture the hammer came with.

4. The resulting texture with the carved hammer is shown in the image.

TEXTURE TIP

Any textures created on metal show up even nicer after applying a patina like liver of sulfur. (See page 45.)

PATINAS

We often think of a patina as the brown or greenish color on statues, but, in fact, patina refers to the film that forms on any surface with the passage of time. While you could make an amulet and wait for time to impart the rich color of age, you can help the process along with the use of chemicals or heat. After a patina is formed on the surface of a piece, darkening it, that surface can be rubbed with a buffing pad, steel wool or very fine sandpaper. The patina gets worn off the high places and remains in the depressions and textured areas much like the action of time and use. There are hundreds of techniques and recipes for the patination of metal and different materials (see Resources, page 140). Here I'm demonstrating two such methods, heat and liver-of-sulfur patina for metal—copper, in this example.

HEAT

1. Heating the metal with a torch is the easiest way to heat patina, but you can also place it in an oven or kiln set to about 400°F. You can even heat it over a stove in a pinch. This example uses sheet metal, but the same methods can be used on wire.

2. Heating begins the patina, but when the object cools, the colors really come out. Rather iridescent colors can be achieved on copper and some other metals, but these colors are often not very permanent. Heating further will produce a darker, more permanent patina.

3. Quenching in water can cause the patina to come off the metal, so you should use a method of cooling called heat-sink cooling. After heating, sandwich the metal between two flat, heavy, metal surfaces. They will quickly cool the piece without loss of color. You can then bring up the high spots as described earlier.

1. Go over your entire piece of metal with a Scotch-Brite pad.

2. If you wish to emboss the piece or add texture, do that now. (See page 41.) Dip the metal into the liver of sulfur. Dip the piece into some warm water and then back into the solution.

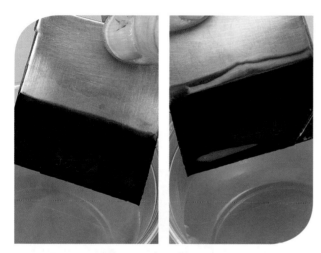

3. Continue until the metal appears as you want it. Generally you want to patina the entire piece, to make sure the piece is fairly even in color and that the recesses are as dark as you want them.

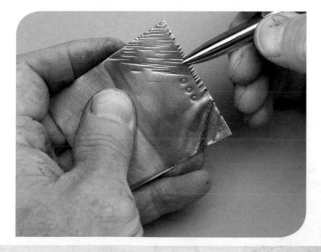

4. If desired, bring up the highlights with a Scotch-Brite pad or steel wool. You can also brass brush the patina right out of the liver of sulfur, yielding a rich, dark brown to black patina.

5. As a final step, you can burnish the edges and/or the high spots and textures with a burnisher to add a bright, reflective "sparkle." The reflection you get by burnishing is the shiniest the metal can get, and it also smoothes the metal better than any other method. For both these reasons, it's a good idea to routinely burnish all edges.

45

CREATIONS

I suppose it may be useful to have definitions for what distinguishes an amulet from a talisman. For the purposes of this book, an amulet is an object—natural or manmade—believed to have the power to protect by magical (versus physical) means. Belief and magic are the salient terms here. The medallion a soccer player wears to stop opponents from kicking him in the shins is an amulet; the shin guard is not.

A talisman needs to be "charged" by the maker or wearer in order to attain its power and is also made for a very specific purpose—at a specific time or place (versus the amulet which is more general and often worn all the time). When an eighth grader takes her lucky pencil, waves it around her head three times, taps it on her head six times and then asks it to mark only the correct answers on the upcoming history test, that pencil becomes a talisman.

The ideas of protection and evocation are often central to the making and wearing of amulets and talismans. They may seem different, but they can be thought of in similar ways. The bushman living on the savanna of Africa may need more rain. Does he make a talisman to ask the gods for rain that afternoon, or does he make an amulet for continual protection from draught? The result may be the same, but the intent during creation is a bit different.

WORKING WITH INTENT

This brings up a very important aspect of making amulets and talismans: working with intent. An essential ingredient to making any amulet, intent can also enhance the making of any artwork and, in fact, of virtually any endeavor. In this book, working with intent has two components: deciding what you want to be the outcome of the work, and being present with the materials, processes and procedures as you move toward that outcome.

Working with intent is more about the non-physical attributes of a work. In "Medal For an Unknown Good Deed" (page 90) for instance, the recognition of what the piece represents is at the heart of the work. It's true that the tin, Faux Bone and riveting are used to bring this recognition into physical existence. However, by actively thinking about the idea of the piece as each component is cut, formed, finished and assembled, it is the idea that steers the work, not the fascination with a material or showing off of a technique.

Intent is extremely important when fashioning amulets, for it is the intent that imbues inanimate objects with power and meaning and allows the user to extract that power. When a mother places herbs, spices, bones and a written prayer in a pouch to hang about her child's neck, the ingredients have no power in and of themselves. It is only by charging these elements with intent that the bag becomes a protective agent for her offspring. Even the ubiquitous rabbit's foot—furry little vessel of good fortune—gains its ability to bring luck only if one is familiar with the myth it embodies and if one invests in a level of belief.

As you go forward to make the projects in this book, I hope you keep the idea of intent in the front of your mind. I hope, too, that you will view the projects as stepping-stones on a path, rather than the final destination. Learning to work with the materials, techniques and procedures in each project will allow you to step off that path and pursue your own trail. This trail will lead you to your final destination—the realization of your artist's voice, which will inform every piece of work you do.

Karma Bracelet

TOOLS

wire cutters

hammer and bench block

tin snips

medium file

400-grit sanding stick

round-nose pliers

chain- or flat-nose pliers

MATERIALS

16-gauge iron wire, four 36" (91cm) lengths

18- and 20-gauge wire for forming hangers and other connectors: copper, sterling silver, iron or similar

tin can, jar or spray paint can

objects of importance to you from your past (old coins, jewelry, charms from trips, relationships, events) to set in tabs, drill holes in, place in bezel cups or use with other settings

images on tin cans, and similar, to cut out

The concept of karma is that the sum of your past actions determines the way of your future and that we keep going around and around until we arrive at our destiny. Though rooted in Hindu and Buddhist philosophy, karma has come to have a much more universal appeal and can be seen as having application in virtually every aspect of the human endeavor. This bracelet is an opportunity for you to include symbols of your past and hopes for your future. You can even make extra loops to add more symbols as your hopes and dreams evolve.

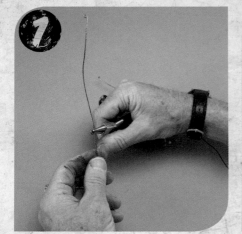

File and sand the ends of one of the 36"
(91cm) wires. Make a loop at each end
of the wire. Make several loops in the
wire about 7" (18cm) apart by holding
the wire with the round-nose pliers and
wrapping the wire once about the pliers
or the barrel of a pen. You can vary your
bracelet by making the loops different
sizes and different lengths apart. Repeat
for all four wires.

Using a spray paint can or similar,
tightly wrap the first wire around the
can. Using pliers, twist each loop so it
faces the outside.

Add on the next wire. Attach the wires
by connecting the end loops.

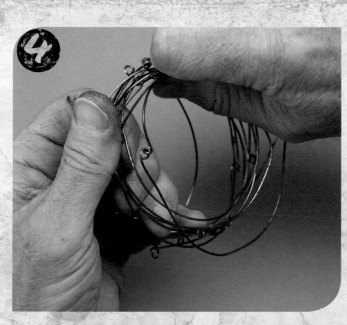

Repeat with the final two wires. When you have finished coiling the wire around, secure the ending loop to any one of the
loops on the rest of the bracelet.

Make charms using found objects, buttons, cut-out tin pieces
or any meaningful objects you may have. Attach the various
charms and objects with jump rings, loops of wire or eye pins,
depending on the elements. Jiggle to let the elements find
their places.

MINKISI

TOOLS

round-nose pliers

small torch

jeweler's saw

bench pin

metal blade, #2/0

medium file

needle tool or awl

hammer

wire cutters

MATERIALS

tea infuser—screen type available at most grocery stores or online

head pins

small beads to act as washers for the head pins

buttons

cannibalized jewelry, beads galore, small shiny objects

objects of meaning for you with a hole or that you can drill a hole into, plus objects to place inside the Minkisi, such as beads, bits of paper, coins, natural materials, spices

18-gauge iron wire or similar

Also called Nkisi, this form of medicine pouch is native to the area of Africa in and around the Congo. Minkisi are usually composed of natural and organic materials combined with personal relics and items of a person's past. Minsiki can be used for protection as we travel into our future or to guard against a specific fear or threat. Seen as "exotic" by some, they are actually very close to many objects used in western religious observations, such as a crucifix or rosary beads. Your Minkisi can protect you from any sort of adversity and can include any items you may choose.

Use heat to patina a mesh tea ball (infuser). I like to hold on to the chain with pliers to make life easier. Be careful not to overheat the mesh, or you could burn a hole in it.

Use a saw to remove the clamp and the bale that came on the ball. (File off the sharp edges.)

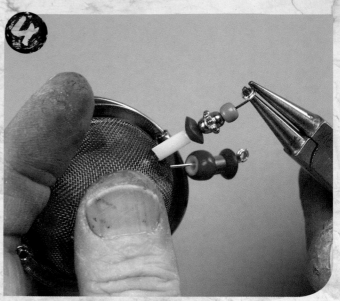

Open up the ball. Use a needle tool at the hinge end of the ball to spread the mesh to create big enough openings for the head pins. Thread a bead onto one pin and then insert it through the ball from the inside to the outside.

On the outside, thread on additional beads (or objects you have drilled holes into) and then make a spiral to secure the beads on the wire.

Repeat to make as many dangles as you wish. Cut two pieces of 18-gauge wire to 4" (10cm). Make a spiral at the end of each wire. Use the needle tool to make a hole at the top of the ball on each half. Bend one spiral so that it is ninety degrees to the rest of the wire. Insert the wire through one hole from the inside of the ball out. Repeat for the other half.

Fill the ball with objects of your choice (be sure to include a secret!).

Close the ball, grasp the two wires together and twist them. Use pliers to make the twist tighter. The twisted portion should be about 2" (5cm) long. Curl the twisted wire down into a bale using round-nose pliers. Finish with a cord or chain of your choice.

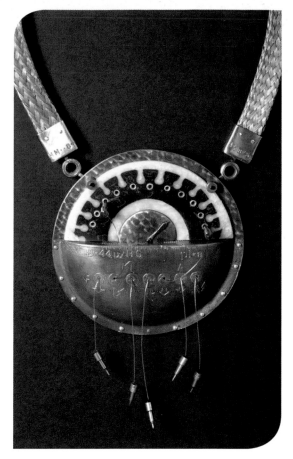

TREBOR'S "S" KEPTIC MONITOR

This piece is a sort of divination tool. The wearer can plug colored pegs into the sterling holes, depending on how she may want her day to proceed. The black and white are a bit like the yin and yang, whereas the white surrounds the black, and vice versa. The pegs are colored, each color symbolizing a mood or a wish.
Etched copper, brass, polymer clay, pen points, epoxy resin, stainless steel, sterling silver

Photo: Douglas Foulke

WARRIORS NECKLACE

PAT GUILLETTE

Sterling silver, copper, patina and colorized pendants, Vermeil, fine silver, old trade beads, turquoise, garnet, copper, amber, pearls, kyanite, citron, lapis, glass seed beads

WABI SABI PENDANT

JENNIFER KAHN

Fine silver, sterling silver, Pyritized ammonite, petrified palmwood

ABRACADABRACUS

TOOLS

tin snips or jeweler's saw and #2/0 blade

bench pin

medium file

medium/fine sandpaper

wire cutters

bench block or similar

cross-peen hammer

drill

#55 drill bit

metal letter stamps

flat-faced hammer

crème brûlée torch

brass brush

chain- and round-nose pliers

MATERIALS

24-gauge brass sheet

pickling solution

19-gauge iron wire, 32" (81cm), cleaned with scouring pad or sandpaper

small glass beads (#9 are what I used here—must fit over 19-gauge wire)

cord or chain for hanging

Abracadabra is one of the oldest, and most famous, written amulets. It was "prescribed" by physicians all the way back to the earliest eras in Roman history. A patient with a cold or fever was instructed to remove a letter each day, and by the time the last letter was deleted, the fever or cold would be magically healed. Of course, the fact that there are eleven letters, and a fever usually lasts a bit over a week…well, you figure it out. The project version is a wearable reminder that an idea need not be true to be real in its effect.

Cut a piece of 24-gauge brass sheet ⅜" × 6½" (1cm × 17cm). With a medium file, file all edges and round the corners. Sand all edges and the rounded corners. Secure the strip in a vise with about ¹⁄₁₆" (2mm) of the strip exposed. Using a cross-peen hammer or the dull blade of a butter knife, "upset" the edge of the strip by hammering the edge with the face of the hammer (or the edge of the knife) at a right angle to the length of the metal strip. Strike only the part of the strip that is held in the vise and move the strip as necessary to upset both sides and the ends.

Beginning at one end of the strip, drill eleven holes, ¼" (6mm) apart using a #55 drill. Repeat on the other end. File and sand any burrs the drill raised in the strip.

To texture the strip, use a metal letter stamp and flat-faced hammer to stamp a design between each hole. (I used the letter X.) Mix up a batch of pickling solution according to the manufacturer's directions and set aside. Heat the strip with a crème brûlée torch until the metal turns a very dull orange.

Allow to cool for a minute and then immerse the strip into the pickle solution for another minute. You will see a bit of a copper and brown/black coating form on the metal. Repeat the heating/quenching process several times until you have a look that suits you.

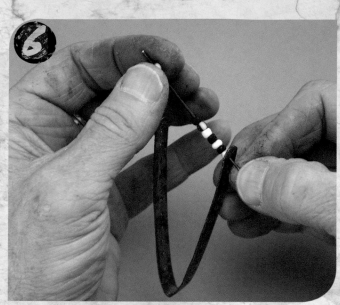

Brush vigorously with a brass brush to bring a soft sheen to the metal. Burnish all the edges. Measure the strip 3¼" (8cm) from one end and mark it. Using chain-nose pliers, grab the strip at the center mark and bend both sides of the strip down.

Cut eleven 2½" (6cm) pieces of 19-gauge iron wire. Take one piece of wire and hammer one end flat using a cross-peen hammer. Thread the wire piece through the bottom hole of the metal strip using the flattened end as a stopper on the outside of the V shape. Thread on eleven beads, alternating the colors.

Insert the opposite end of the wire through the opposite hole and trim the protruding wire to ⅛" (3mm). Using the cross-peen hammer, hammer the extending section to form another stopper. Repeat for the next piece of wire, this time threading ten beads onto it and repeat again with nine beads on the third wire.

Again, after the beads are on, trim the wire, leaving ⅛" (3mm) and splay the end with a cross-peen hammer.

TURN OFF THE SHINE

If you prefer your beads to be less shiny, immerse them in Armour Etch solution to make them as matte as you'd like before threading onto the wires. To add a bit of age to the beads after etching, apply a small amount of brown shoe polish with a short bristle brush, allow to dry and rub the pile of beads in a soft cloth.

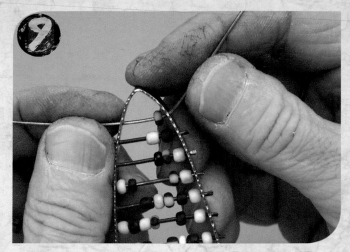

Continue hammering and threading the wires for the seven rows, subtracting one bead on each row and finishing with two beads on the second-from-the-top wire. To finish the beading, cut a 4" (10cm) piece of 19-gauge iron wire. Clean the wire and file the ends. Thread it through the top hole with a single bead in the middle.

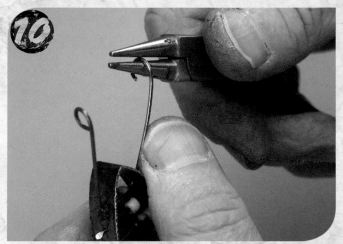

Using your hands, turn both sides of the wire up. Using round-nose pliers, create a loop on both ends.

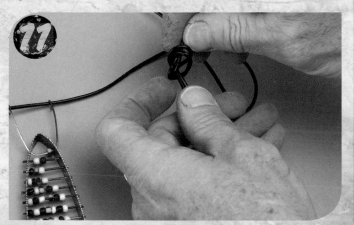

Thread a length of black leather cord (or cord of your choice) through the loops and knot it.

GRID FIGURE #43C

Sterling silver, polymer clay, turquoise, freshwater pearl

PRAYER HOLDER BRACELET

TOOLS

wire cutters

flat-faced hammer

medium file

jeweler's saw

Faux Bone blade, medium

metal blade, #2/0

bench pin

cross-peen hammer

drill or pin vise

1/16" (2mm) drill bit

awl, scribe or craft knife

cut-off bristle brush

round-faced hammer

silicon carbide (wet/dry) sandpaper, grits 320, 400, 600

chain-nose pliers

MATERIALS

18-gauge wire, 45" (114cm)

16-gauge wire, 4" and 3" (10cm and 8cm)

spray paint can or something with a similar diameter

3/4" (19mm) PVC tubing, 1½"(4cm) long

Faux Bone shaving tool

24-gauge sheet metal

acrylic paint or shoe polish

written prayer or other object to be contained within the tube

Women (and sometimes men) from various cultures wear pieces of jewelry that contain "prayers" of different sorts. The containers for these prayers range from Coptic snakeskin vials to sterling silver boxes and tubes, and are used by both Christian and Muslim religions. What is contained in this jewelry varies just as much. Sometimes it is a prayer for the protection of a child, sometimes a section of the Koran or perhaps a plea for deliverance from adversity.

What you insert into your bracelet is up to you and can take any form you deem proper. Address any idea, feeling or desire you choose. I have made these for friends experiencing a difficult time or dealing with a loss of some kind, and I find that my focus on something outside myself often informs the designs that decorate the container.

Cut 45" (114cm) of 18-gauge copper wire. Using an old flat-faced hammer, hammer the wire to texture it. (An old hammer will leave more of an interesting texture, as will the uneven surface of the side of your anvil.) File the ends of the wire.

SOME LIKE IT ROUGH

If you can get an old hammer, you can texture the wire completely. You can do this by turning the wire regularly but randomly while hammering, and by hammering on a rough surface such as concrete or the side of an anvil.

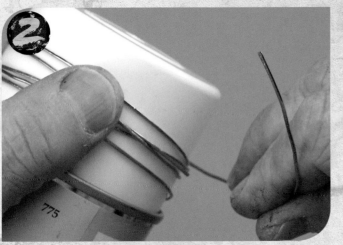

Using a spray paint can, tightly wrap the wire around it.

Using a jeweler's saw and a Faux Bone blade (or pipe cutter), cut a 1½" (4cm) piece of ¾" (19mm) PVC pipe.

MEDITATION RING

JENNIFER KAHN

Inspired by Tibetan singing bowls, used for meditation.
Fine silver, 24-karat gold

LET'S GET THIS STRAIGHT

Here's a super trick for using paper as a guide while drawing a straight line around a cylinder. Bring the ends of the paper evenly together. When the paper lines up, draw your circle along the edge of the paper.

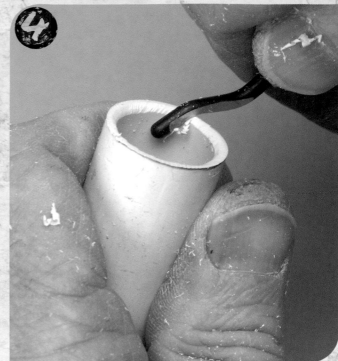

File the ends of the PVC tube square. Use the Faux Bone forming tool (or the round side of a half-round file) to smooth and bevel the inside of the pipe's edges.

Trace two 1" (3cm) circles onto 24-gauge copper sheet. Using a cross-peen hammer, texture the circles. Using a $\frac{1}{16}$" (2mm) drill bit, drill a hole in the center of each circle. Using a jeweler's saw and a metal blade (or tin snips), cut out the disks from the sheet. Place one disk into the largest hole in the dapping block and use a round-face hammer to shape the disk.

Cut a 4" (10cm) piece of 16-gauge copper wire. Bend it into a U shape. Using a flat-faced hammer, flatten the bend.

Measure in ½" (12mm) from both ends of the PVC tube and mark. Using a ¹⁄₁₆" (2mm) drill bit, start at the marks and drill straight down through the other side of the tube.

Use a file, carving tool, craft knife, electric etcher or other tool to scratch designs into the surface of the tube. Sand the surface to remove burrs and impart a shine to the surface. Finish with shoe polish (see Sanding and Polishing, page 35).

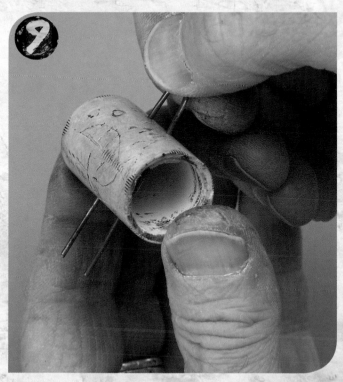

Patina the U-shaped wire (see Patinas, page 44). Insert the U-shaped wire into the PVC tube.

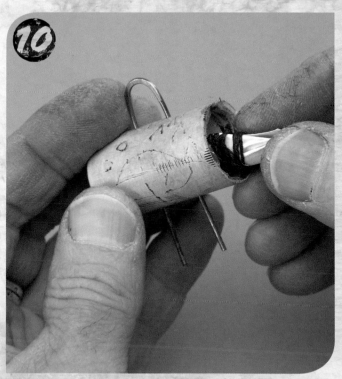

Prepare a prayer or intention on a piece of paper, wrap the paper with red waxed linen and insert it into the bead, or merely speak the prayer or intention into the bead.

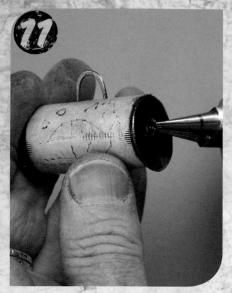

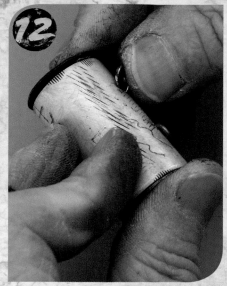

Cut a 3" (8cm) piece of 16-gauge copper wire and make a loop on one end. Patina the wire. Thread one of the metal disks onto the wire and then thread the wire through the tube and through the other disk. Coil the end of the wire to secure the disks to the bead.

Spiral the excess shafts of the U-shaped wire and fold it against the bead.

Patina the wire coil using liver of sulfur.

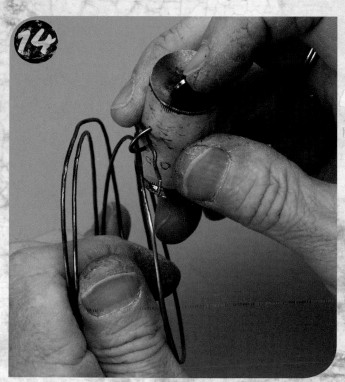

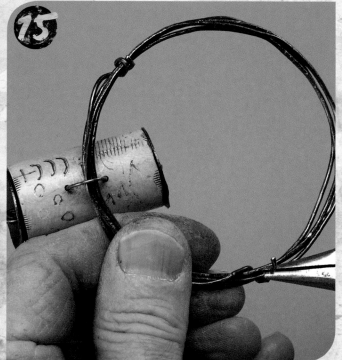

Thread the bead onto one end of the coil, making sure to pick up the beginning of the coil at every rotation.

When the bead has fully attached to the wire, curl the two wire ends around the coil to secure the bracelet, using chain-nose pliers to crimp with.

SAUN BEAD #6

This is a tube bead with a prayer housed inside. The word *Saun* is a reference to a fictitious culture made up as part of a personal myth. Because it is for a woman, I used silver—traditionally and symbolically considered feminine in character.

Faux Bone, sterling silver, rutilated quartz, pearls

MAMMA, DID YOU SING?

DONNA PENOYER

This whistle ring is for a friend who set aside her dreams to take care of her family. I envisioned a touchstone that would call her back to her song and tried to make it irresistible and proud. In my talismanic scenario, her children and their question are the only things powerful enough to reawaken her.

Metal clay

TIBETAN PRAYER WHEEL

ANGELA BAUSUEL-CRISPIN

Metal clay, Faux Bone, brass, gold, paper

BOUND HEART PENDANT

The heart is perhaps one of the most common and overused symbols in our culture (and others). However, that also makes it potentially very powerful. Originally the heart was a symbol for life. Only recently has it come to symbolize love. For this project, I like the play on the duality of the idea of being "bound." Does the wire restrict the heart, keep it from coming apart, or is the wire surrounding the heart, keeping it safe? Are all the "attachments" remembrances of good times gone by, mementos of a failed relationship or items to spark the imagination about what is yet to come?

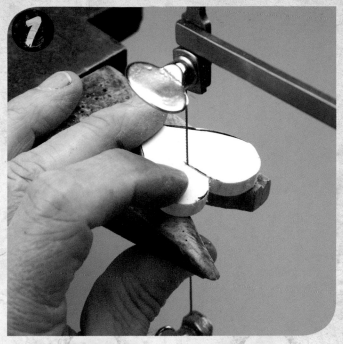

On the Faux Bone sheet, draw a heart that is a bit off center and has different size lobes at the top. At the point where the lobes meet, continue the line of one of the lobes about ½" (12mm) into the middle of the heart. Cut the heart out, using the saw, cutting the line that continues the lobe as well. This is where the lobes will bend apart.

File, sand and polish the heart (see Sanding and Polishing, page 35). Using the heat gun, heat the heart from below in the area between the lobes. Heat from one side and then the other until it is very malleable.

Bend the lobes away from each other, one toward the back, and one toward the front.

Submerge the heart in water, and it will lock into position immediately. If you like the form, keep it, or you can reheat it and it will go back to its original flat form and you can shape it again. This can be repeated as many times as you like. Texture and color the heart as you like using marking tools and acrylic paint or shoe polish and a cut-off bristle brush (see Surface Textures, page 41). Using a #54 drill bit, drill a hole in the top of the lobe you want your pendant to hang from. Drill two more holes with a #55 drill bit, one on each side of the heart.

Cut 1" (3cm) of 16-gauge copper wire and make an eye pin (see Eye Pins, page 24). Put a dot of Zap-A-Gap glue at the end of the eye pin and insert it into the hole on the top of the large lobe.

Cut a 24" (61cm) piece of 19-gauge iron wire and clean it (sand it with sandpaper). Make a right-angle bend at one end of the wire, put a dot of Zap-A-Gap on the tip and stick it in one of the lower holes.

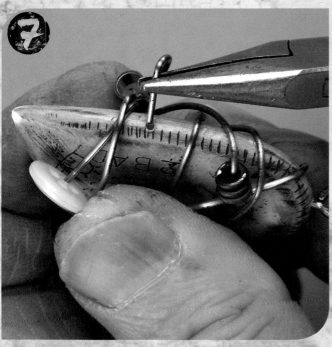

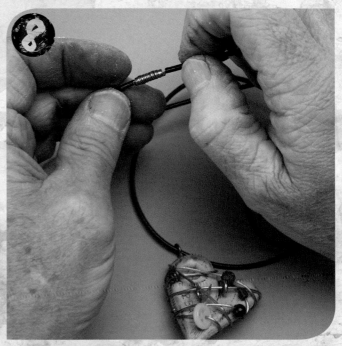

Add beads as you randomly wrap the wire in different directions around the heart. Make sure you have enough wire to go past the last hole. With the wire over the hole, trim it to ½" (12mm) beyond the hole. Bend it at a right angle, put a dot of glue on the tip and insert it into the hole.

Measure a length of leather cord and thread it through the eye. Make a ½" (12mm) coil out of clean, flattened iron wire (see Wire Coils, page 22). Insert the ends of the cord into the coil and crimp the ends of the coil.

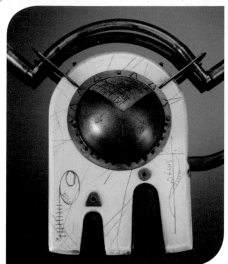 

DOUBLE HEART MONITOR FOR MILAN

Milan was my father, who died of a heart attack many years ago. I made this monitor and "gave" it to him symbolically. My hope is that he can use it to avoid the same fate wherever he may be now.

Copper, Faux Bone, polymer clay, surgical tubing, brass

JOURNEY NECKLACE

JENNIFER KAHN

From found objects collected on my travels.

Fine silver, serpentine, shell, button, ammonite

EQUIVOQUE BRACELET (FOR THE CARPENTER'S WIFE)

The triangle is the symbol of both male and female, depending on which way the point is oriented. I was thinking here of a man and woman building a life together, hence the carpenter's rule as the material and the bracelet as the form. The copper is used as the core of the piece, as it is traditionally the metal that symbolizes love and harmony.

Antique carpenter's rule, copper, brass

RUNE NECKLACE

TOOLS

craft knife or scalpel

round-nose pliers

scribe, awl or needle tool

medium file

silicon carbide (wet and dry)
sandpaper

jeweler's saw

metal blade, #2/0

bench pin

MATERIALS

polymer clay, ecru and black
(or any two contrasting colors)

paper and pen for designing
your runes

18-gauge wire

⅛" (3mm) brass tubing, 3" (8cm)

acrylic paint

cyanoacrylate glue
(like Zap-a-Gap)

cord for hanging

OPTIONAL

pasta machine for
conditioning clay

checkering file

shoe polish

Runes were originally letters from the earliest Germanic alphabets but have become more commonly known as marks of mysterious or magical significance. They are often seen in sets in which you ask a question, select one rune, consult the corresponding written oracle and apply it to whatever question you may have posited before your selection. You can, however, select a number of runes and construct a series of guiding principles. For this necklace, I went one step further and designed my own rune symbols. I encourage you to do the same and even write down the principles they may represent. In this way, your necklace can act as a reminder of ideals and values you hold important.

Condition one half of a package of ecru polymer clay and one quarter of a package of black (see page 36). Divide the ecru clay into five equal sections. Form the clay into basic stone shapes—they need not be identical. Sketch out your chosen runes and begin transferring them to the clay. You can either do this freehand or you can put the sketch on top of the clay and lightly retrace the design and it will transfer an indentation to the clay.

After the basic sketches are on your five pieces of clay, use a wire or the back of a craft-knife blade to define and deepen the design indentations.

Cut two 1" (3cm) pieces of 18-gauge wire. Create a loop on the end of each using round-nose pliers to create an eye pin. Use the pliers to create texture along the length and around the loop of the pins.

Insert the pins into the top of one rune, ½" (12mm) apart so the eye is just meeting the clay. Repeat for the remaining rune beads.

Divide the black clay into six portions. To create spacer beads, form each into an oblong shape and insert a needle tool through the entire shape. Insert it from both ends and then roll along your work surface to even out the shape.

Poke several holes over the surface of the bead to be inlaid later. Repeat for the other five spacer beads and bake all the ecru runes and black beads, according to package directions.

Inlay cooled ecru runes with the black clay, and the black beads with the ecru clay. Bake to cure (see Inlaying, page 37). Once the pieces have cooled, file the excess clay from the surface of each piece and sand and polish with silicon carbide sandpaper as desired (see Sanding and Polishing, page 35).

Texture the brass tubing by scraping a checkering file or regular file along the length of it.

Cut the tubing into six ½"(12mm) lengths and verify that each fits between the two eye pins on each rune. The tubing may be given a patina with a torch at this point.

Texture and color the runes, too, if you like, using acrylic paint or shoe polish and a soft brush (see Surface Textures, page 41). Remove the eye pins, add a dot of glue to the shaft and reinsert into the rune. Note that you should position the opening of the eye pin at the back of the runes. Begin threading the beads onto the cord, starting with a black bead. Next, thread on a rune, with a copper pipe segment between the eye loops, and then a black bead, and so forth. Finish the necklace with a coiled-wire clasp (see Hook and Latch Clasps, page 25).

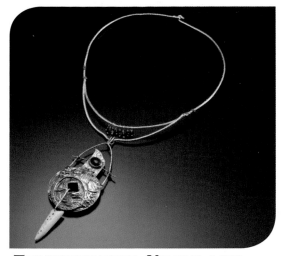

THUNDERBIRD NECKLACE

PAT GUILLETTE

Fine silver, 24-karat gold Keum-boo, stamped sterling silver, carved bone, gold-filled wire, tourmaline, peridot, glass seed beads, forged/stamped sterling neck ring

ROUND LOCKET

CELIE FAGO

This metal locket surrounds a shred of paper which contained in this small, durable shrine, becomes something so ephemeral— a testament to our vulnerability. *Fine silver, paper, polymer clay, sterling chain and hinge pin*

BUDDHA NECKLACE

JENNIFER KAHN

Fine silver, bronze, sterling beads, Peruvian opal

ANTI-WAR MEDAL #3

LINDA KAYE-MOSES

Sterling and fine silver, 18-karat gold, amethyst, moonstone, shell, freshwater pearls, polymer clay

PROTECTION FOR THE TRAVELER

TOOLS

jeweler's saw
Faux Bone blade, fine
metal blade, #2/0
bench pin
half-round file, medium
sanding stick or sandpaper
checkering file
letter stamps or other metal stamps
bench block
flat-head hammer
mallet or dead-blow hammer
wood block
drill
1/16" (2mm) drill bit
wire cutters
round-nose pliers
brass brush

MATERIALS

1/16" (2mm) Faux Bone
24-gauge copper or similar
#0-80 micro bolts and nuts
18-gauge copper wire
patina materials
5mm x 12mm bullet-shaped stone or similar
rusted washer or similar

OPTIONAL

tin snips

Eyes are a traditional symbol for protection when traveling. To this day, in many European countries, eyes can be found painted on the front of boats, cars and even airplanes, presumably enabling the vehicle and passenger to find the way home. The washer at the top of this amulet is my symbol for an eye, and the wings are to ensure the swift completion of the trip.

This particular talisman was made for a friend deathly afraid of flying, hence the repeated inscription: "The plane will stay up." This is her personal mantra when flying. The carnelian, traditionally associated with the third eye, is to afford her peace of mind.

Cut a piece of Faux Bone to about 2½" × 1½" (6cm × 4cm). Draw a set of connected wings on the Faux Bone and cut out with a jeweler's saw equipped with a fine Faux Bone blade (see Faux Bone and Plexiglas, page 33).

On a piece of 24-gauge copper, draw an oval approximately 1" × 2" (3cm × 5cm). Draw a ⅜" (10mm) circle about ⅛" (3mm) in from one end of the oval. Drill a small hole inside the circle and cut it out with a jeweler's saw and metal blade (see Piercing a Window, page 32).

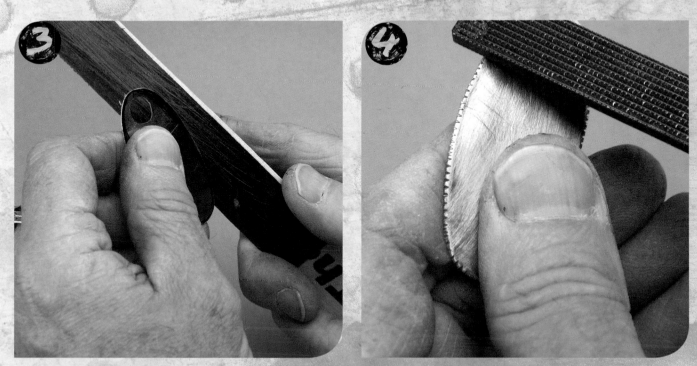

Using a jeweler's saw or tin snips, saw or cut out the larger shape of the oval. File the edge of the oval to refine the shape. Sand the edges using sandpaper or a sanding stick.

If you like, use a checkering file to create texture around the edge of the oval.

Using ⅛" (3mm) metal letter stamps and a flat-head hammer, place the oval on the anvil and stamp it with words.

On a block of wood, create a dap by making a large diameter indentation with a hammer (see page 105). Using a dead-blow hammer or rawhide mallet, curve the oval by hammering it from the back into the depression in the jig.

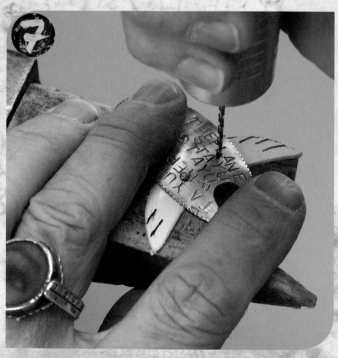

Position the wings beneath the oval and about one-third down from the top (the end with the hole). Using a ¹⁄₁₆" (2mm) drill bit, drill one hole on one side of the oval and the wings. Insert a bolt to keep the pieces in place. Repeat with the other side of the oval. Remove the nut, bolt and wings.

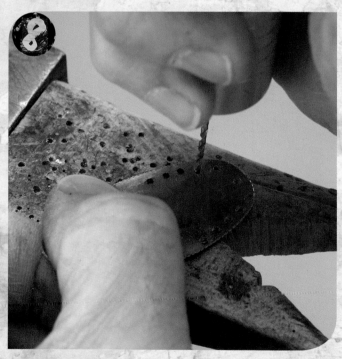

Using a ¹⁄₁₆" (2mm) drill bit, drill a total of eleven holes (one at the bottom and five up each side), approximately ⅛" (3mm) apart.

Make a coil of 18-gauge copper wire. Hold the wire on the round-nose pliers and distress the coils with a checkering file. Make ten jump rings (see Jump Rings, page 23). Attach one to each of the five holes on the sides.

Mix a batch of liver of sulfur according to the manufacturer's directions and patina the oval and jump rings to the desired color. Brass brush all the parts to a soft sheen and burnish all edges.

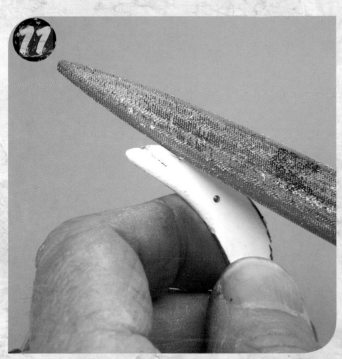

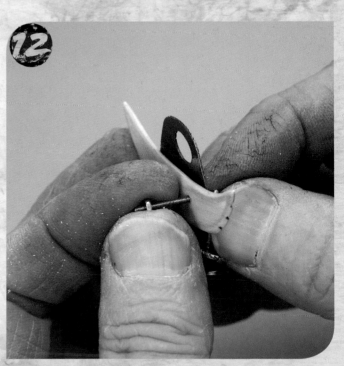

File and sand the edges of the wings. Using the edge of the half-round file, create the lines of the feathers. Tilt the file at an angle to round the front more than the back.

Add color to the wings (see Faux Bone, page 41) and any other texture as desired. Reattach the wings to the metal oval using the nuts and bolts. Trim the excess shaft of the bolts and rivet.

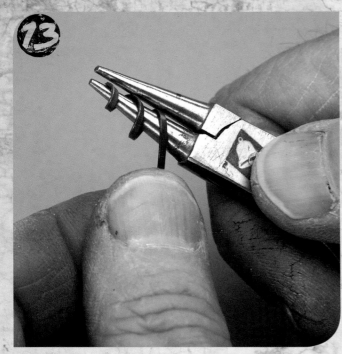

Cut a 5" (13cm) piece of 18-gauge wire and flatten it using a flat-faced hammer. Spiral the wire down one prong of the round-nose pliers.

Take the wire off the pliers and bend it back onto itself. Grasp the wire at the bend and bend it again at the pliers' edge. Cut the wire ¾" (19mm) above the last bend and form a loop in the wire.

Insert the bullet stone into the spiral and twist the wire spiral around the stone to tighten if needed. Insert the loop at the top of the spiral into the hole at the bottom of the oval and twist the loop closed.

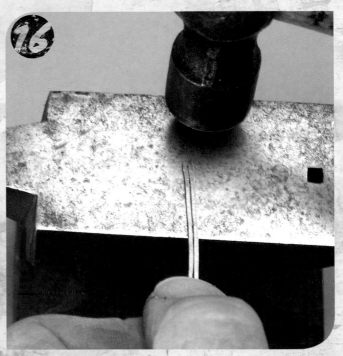

Cut an 8" (20cm) piece of 18-gauge wire and fold it in half. Pinch the open end tightly with pliers and use a flat-faced hammer to hammer the wire flat.

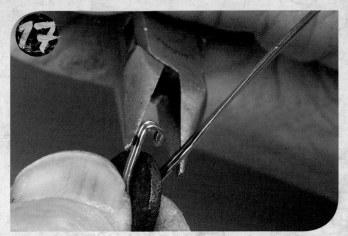

Use heat to patina the wire, and then use a brass brush to polish the wire. Grasping the folded end with chain-nose pliers, create a tiny hook. About ½" (12mm) from the hook, create another bend in the same direction. Thread on the washer and squeeze the wire to secure the washer.

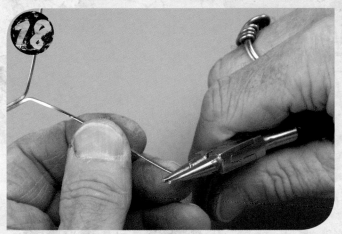

At ½" (12mm) above where the hook goes over the washer, grasp the wire with a pair of chain-nose pliers and separate the wires into a Y shape. About 1" (3cm) from the separation, give the wires a one-quarter turn to create a slight twist. Using round-nose pliers, make a loop on the ends of both wires.

Cut a 1" (3cm) piece of 18-gauge wire and clean and patina it. Also patina the Y bail. Bend the 1" (3cm) wire to form an oblong jump ring. Connect the oval and the washer using the jump ring. Attach a chain to the loops of the Y bail.

RITUAL SHIELD BROOCH

PAT GUILLETTE

24-karat gold, 18-karat gold, fine silver, sterling silver, colorization (acrylic and Prismacolor pencils), brass, sugilite, turquoise

LAIBON AX PENDANT

TOOLS

permanent marker

jeweler's saw

Faux Bone blade, medium

metal blade, #2/0

bench pin

medium file

silicone carbide (wet/dry)
sandpaper, grits 320, 400, 600

drill or pin vise

1/16" (2mm) drill bit

#54 drill bit

marking tools such as metal stamps,
scribe, nail set, center punch

cut-off bristle brush

wire cutters

small torch

round-nose pliers

hammer

square-nose pliers

MATERIALS

1/4" (6mm) Faux Bone

epoxy putty

paint

shoe polish

18-gauge copper wire

OPTIONAL

1" (3cm) stationary belt sander

Faux Bone shaping tool

The bladelike form of this piece is truly archetypal. It is found in most cultures in various applications. In Spanish cooking it is a *mezza luna* (half moon) and used for chopping food. In early America it was called a skive and used for leatherworking. In some west coast African countries, it was made into a ring and used as a weapon. Hung about the neck, it is common for protection from evil spirits (illness) that may try to enter the chest cavity.

As is common with this sort of style of amulet, the blade protects, and the beads surrounding it amplify the power of the central element.

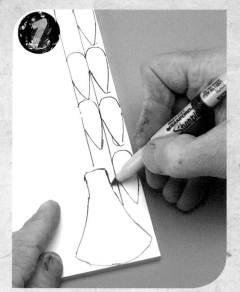

On a ¼" (6mm) piece of Faux Bone, sketch out the pieces of your amulet, using a permanent marker. Here I am creating an ax shape, along with six amplifier shapes that are toothlike in shape.

Use a saw to cut the shapes apart. When you have multiple identical shapes, it makes life easier if you line them up in a strip and work off the strip as much as possible.

In lieu of a belt sander (see Belt Sander, page 35), a file can be used to shape the Faux Bone as you like it.

After drawing where you would like an inlay on your pendant, cut the shape or shapes out with the saw. The wedge shapes here are designed to echo the shapes in the amplifier beads.

Mix up some two-part putty epoxy (see package directions) and push it into the areas you wish to inlay.

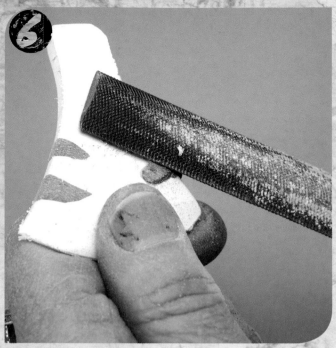

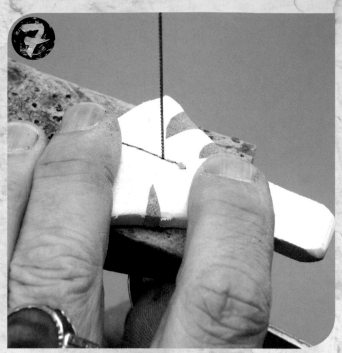

Pack the cutouts so that a bit of putty is above the surface of the Faux Bone in both the front and the back. Set aside to cure. When fully cured, file off the putty down to the surface of the Faux Bone to reveal the inlay.

Here, for added interest, I drilled a small hole up about 1" (3cm) from the center of the blade of the ax. I then drew a line from the hole to the edge of the blade and then cut a slit through the bone from the hole, outward.

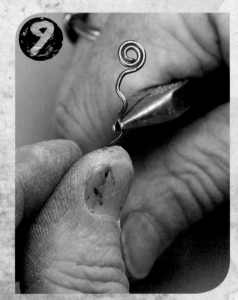

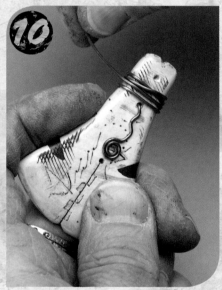

Decorate your pieces as desired using marking tools, shoe polish and a cut-off bristle brush (see Surface Textures, page 41). Drill one hole from front to back about ¼" (6mm) down from the top edge and centered in the width of the piece. Drill another hole ½" (13mm) down from the first. Holes in the smaller pieces should be the same; however, the second hole should be ¼" (6mm) down from the first.

Cut an 18" (96cm) length of 18-gauge wire. Patina the wire with a torch. Create a spiral at one end of the wire, and then a wavy line using round-nose pliers.

Insert the wire through the bottom of the two holes just drilled, from the front to the back. Bend the wavy-wire portion down and flat against the ax. Begin wrapping the wire around the upper portion of the ax.

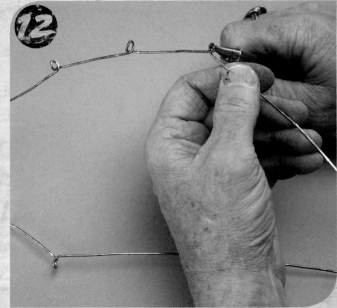

Continue wrapping the wire until you have about 4" (10cm) left. Insert the tail through the top hole, pull it snuggly and hammer the remainder flat. Use round-nose pliers to loop the wire and coil it down to make a bale. Cut six 12" (30cm) lengths of 18-gauge wire. Create identical or varying types of spirals on each and repeat the wrapping process on each of the smaller pieces.

Cut 30" (76cm) of 16-gauge wire and bend the wire in half. Grasp the bend with the round-nose pliers and twist it twice. Measure 2" (5cm) from the loop, grasp the wire with the round-nose pliers and fold the wire in half. Grasp the wire at the folded mark and cross the wire lengths under the loop made by the pliers. Still grasping the loop, turn the loop one-quarter turn. This makes the loop perpendicular to the main wire. Repeat this process two more times on the same side and then three times on the opposite side of the center loop.

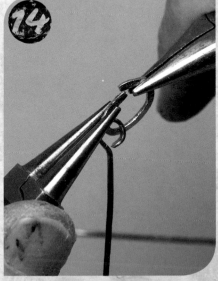

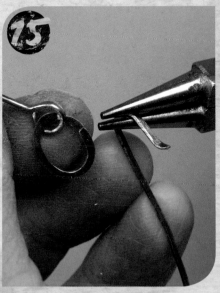

Create seven jump rings from 18-gauge wire. (See Jump Rings, page 23.) Use one jump ring to connect each piece to one loop in the wire, created in the previous step.

At one end of the wire, create an eye loop with round-nose pliers. Make a single large jump ring and hammer it flat. Connect it to the eye loop.

Flatten about ¾" (19mm) of the end of the other wire and make a small crook in it with round-nose pliers. Bend the wire into a hook to complete.

THE PROTECTIVE EYE

TOOLS

photocopy from an older copy machine (carbon toner type) and extra scrap paper

scissors

clay roller

oval template

jeweler's saw

metal blade, #2/0

Faux Bone blade, medium

bench pin

cut-off bristle brush

permanent marker

metal stamps

checkering file

drill

#55 drill bit

1/8" (3mm) drill bit

triangular scraper

flat-faced hammer

eyelet setter

bench block

medium file

cross-peen hammer

round-nose pliers

chain-nose or square-nose pliers

MATERIALS

polymer clay, light color such as transparent, white, ecru or ivory

shoe polish

24-gauge sheet metal

16-gauge wire nails or brads

1/8" (3mm) eyelets

As in Protection for the Traveler (page 72), the eye here is protective, but in a different way. As in most cultures where the "evil eye" (actually a positive element for the wearer) is present, wearing an eye has two functions. The first is to distract negative energy as it approaches you and the second is to stare the bad energy down and turn it away. To make this a true talisman, you can think of "charging" it by thinking of specific protections you may need as you make it. You can ask for protection from an occurrence (failing a test for instance) or you can enlist the talisman to ensure success (please help me to get an A+ on my test). This one was made for a friend who had just lost a loved one, hence the "holes" in the bottom to symbolize the emptiness she felt. The texture created with the letter C is to help her "see" her way through her situation and not succumb to the negative energy of loss.

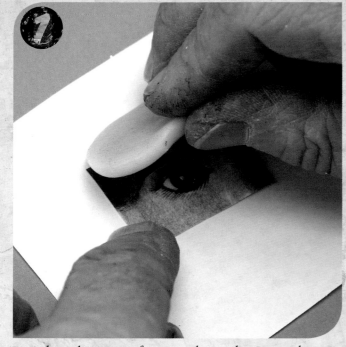

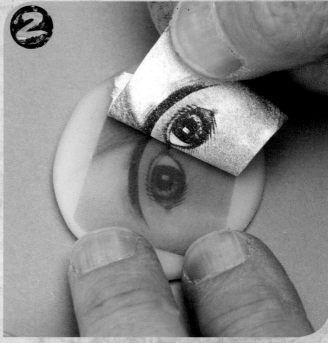

Begin by making a transfer onto polymer clay. Start with a copy from a toner-based copier (the older, slower machines are the best) that is the size you want. Using scissors, trim the eye including a bit of room around the edge. Place faceup on a piece of scrap paper. Pinch out a piece of conditioned clay (see page 36) so that it's just large enough to cover the image. Push the clay onto a smooth, clean piece of scrap paper and peel it up checking to make sure there are no dents in the clay's surface. If it looks good, press it onto the copy and roll the clay to a thickness of ⅛" (3mm). With the clay sitting on top of the image, bake the clay at 225°F for about 45 minutes.

When the piece has finished baking and cooled, gently peel up the copy to reveal the transfer.

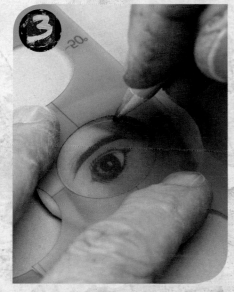

Use an oval template to trace a penciled line around the portion of the transfer you want to use.

Cut the piece out using a Faux Bone blade.

Use a cut-off bristle brush and a bit of shoe polish to age the edges of the clay piece.

Trace the clay piece onto 24-gauge metal sheet, using a permanent marker. Using the same marker, draw in four small tabs. You may wish to try this on a scrap of paper first and cut it out to make certain your tabs are long enough to fold over the piece of clay.

Cut the piece out with a jeweler's saw and a metal blade. Next, cut a square or rectangle—from the metal sheet—that is larger than and proportionate to your tab setting. Add texture, such as the letter C I'm using here. Add texture to the edges, too, if you like, like I did with the checkering file.

Patina both the rectangle and the tab setting, using the method of your choice. Mark three holes on the tab setting, creating a triangle, with the apex at the top of the setting. Drill the three holes using a #55 bit. Place the tab setting over the rectangle piece where you want it and drill one hole through the rectangle at one of the holes in the tab setting. Set in a temporary nail, drill the second hole and repeat for the third and final hole. Remove the nails. Use a triangular scraper (or drill bit slightly larger than the holes) to bevel the three holes in the tab setting.

Drill three ⅛" (3mm) holes along the bottom edge of the rectangle. Set an eyelet in each hole. File the heads of three nails flat. Set the two rivets that are side by side. Cut a strip of metal sheet to 1" × ¼" (3cm × 6mm). Leaving about ½" (13mm) flat at one end, create a full loop with round-nose pliers. File the edges and the corners of the flat portion. At about ⅜" (10mm) from the end, drill a hole with the #55 bit. Patina the bale. Set the bale in the remaining hole with the third nail, using a cross-peen hammer to avoid hitting the loop.

Set the clay piece into the tab setting. Working gradually in a circular motion, cinch in the tabs to secure the piece, using the side of a pair of square- or chain-nose pliers. Thread whatever chain or cord you like through the bale to finish.

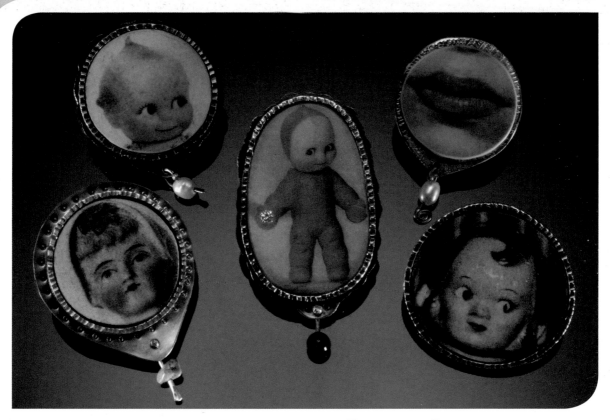

POLYMER CLAY
IMAGE TRANSFER PINS

Each pin is a symbol for a childhood memory. The center piece refers to my growing up near the Coney Island amusement park, where Kewpie Dolls were given as prizes. This doll holds my sparkling memory of those times, in her hand, and the undulating edge is how my tummy felt after all the rides.

Polymer clay with photo transfer, sterling silver, cubic zirconia, pearls, turquoise, carnelian

SMALL LOCKET WITH
POLYMER INLAY

CELIE FAGO

Textures on this piece derive from ancient and modern languages—foreign, familiar, alive and passed—including Latin and Linear B, Sumerian and Greek, Italian and Chinese. Together, this expresses my impulse toward homogeneity, a unity and a palimpsest; a personal talisman of hope for the human story.

Fine silver, sterling silver, plymer clay, gold-leaf 2000

Story Bracelet

TOOLS

permanent marker

straightedge

compass

drill or pin vise

$\frac{1}{16}$" (2mm) drill bit

jeweler's saw

Faux Bone blade, medium

Faux Bone shaping tool

triangular scraper

medium file

silicone carbide (wet/dry) sandpaper, grits 320, 400, 600

electric etcher or pointed scribe

checkering file

round-nose pliers

chain-nose pliers

MATERIALS

$\frac{1}{8}$" (3mm) Faux Bone, 4" × 4" (10cm × 10cm)

acrylic paint

16-gauge wire

found objects for charms such as potsherds, bottle caps, images cut from tin cans, coins, buttons, reflectors, washers, rusty bits of metal, parts of model cars, old jewelry parts, etc.

The design for this piece came from combining the format of a traditional charm bracelet with the idea of a journal. I view the collecting of charms as a way of marking the passage of time with objects that symbolize people, events or places. This is much like writing about them in a journal to help you remember them. In this bracelet, you can write about a subject directly on the Faux Bone and then surround the writing with symbols that reflect the same. Or you can begin with the symbols and write about them. The choice, as always, is yours.

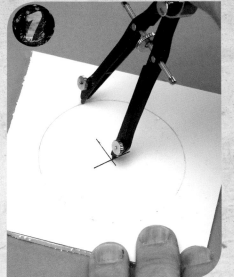

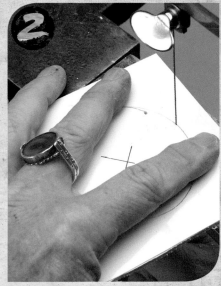

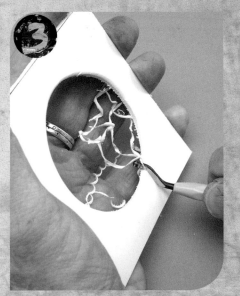

Using a permanent marker and a straightedge, find the center of the piece of Faux Bone by positioning the straightedge from corner to corner and making an X in the center where the lines cross. Position your compass with the point on the center of the X and draw a 2½" (6cm) circle (smaller or larger, as your hand may require). Alternately you can draw any shape for the hole you want. Square holes need a smaller opening because the hand is inserted diagonally through the hole.

Drill a hole just inside the circle line. Using a jeweler's saw and a Faux Bone blade, cut out the circle.

Using the shaping tool or the round side of a half-round file, round over the edges on both sides of the cutout, yielding a smooth, slightly beveled edge.

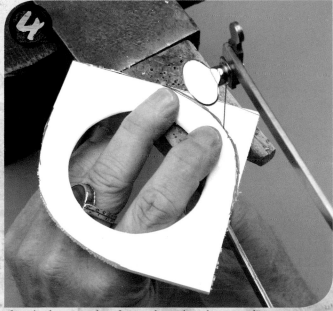

Sketch the outside of your bracelet shape with a permanent marker. This can be any shape you like. Use the saw to cut this out as well.

File the outside to smooth out the cut line. Decide where you want holes for your charms and mark for them around the outside of the bracelet. This does not have to be measured or evenly spaced; they can be anywhere on the bracelet. Drill a ¹⁄₁₆" (2mm) hole at each mark.

Now take a triangular scraper (or drill bit that is slightly larger than the drilled holes) and bevel the drilled holes on both sides of the bracelet. This gives a more finished look and allows for better motion of the jump rings and wires from which your charms will hang.

Wet sand the bracelet with 400-grit sandpaper. Use an etching tool or sharp scribe to create your story all around both sides of your bracelet. Your story can consist of words, textures, symbols or any combination of these. It might be interesting to try some automatic writing or some other method of generating your story.

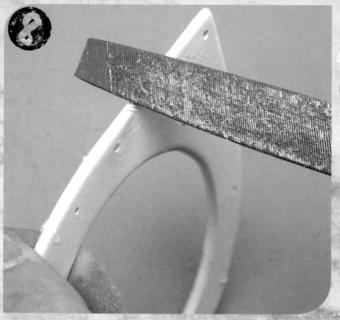

With 600-grit sandpaper, sand off the burrs created from the etching. Add texture using files such as a checkering file. This can be done along the outer edge of the bracelet as well. Here, I made small notches.

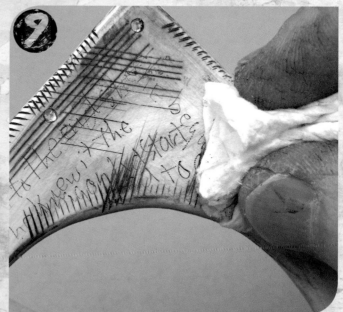

Rub acrylic paint into the bracelet and then rub the excess off. (See Surface Textures, page 41.) Use as many or as few colors as you like.

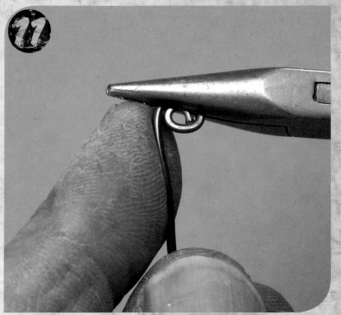

When the bracelet is colored and polished as you'd like, it's time to add your charms. To create your own jump rings, first decide on a color of 16-gauge wire. I like to use copper, but I also like to heat-patina it first. Create several jump rings (see Jump Rings, page 23). If you wish to use an object as a charm that doesn't have a hole in it, you can make your own hole using a drill with a 1/16" (2mm) bit.

As an alternative to using jump rings, you can create a spiral on one end of a 4" (10cm) length of wire. Begin with a small loop. Use chain-nose pliers to form a spiral around the loop.

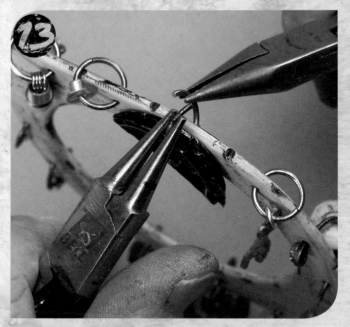

Thread the tail end of the wire through a hole in the bracelet and then thread your chosen bead or object. Create a second loop or small spiral at the other end of the object.

To add objects with jump rings, use two pairs of pliers to open the jump ring, thread it onto the bracelet, thread on your bead or object and then use both pliers to close the jump ring.

MEDAL FOR AN UNKNOWN GOOD DEED

TOOLS

jeweler's saw

metal blade, #2/0

Faux Bone blade, medium

bench pin

medium or fine file

drill

#55 drill bit

round-nose pliers

square-nose pliers

wire cutters

round-face hammer

MATERIALS

tin from a can, container
or other source

⅛" (3mm) Faux Bone,
small piece, approximately
1½" × 2" (4cm × 5cm)

scrap wood

16-gauge wire for rivets and eye
pins OR wire nails or headpins

19-gauge steel wire, 10" (25cm)

OPTIONAL

tin snips

washers, beads, buttons
or any small dangles
with holes in them

You have, at some time, performed a good deed for someone else simply because you thought it was the right thing to do. You weren't looking to be rewarded or singled out for this action; it was enough to just do it. I rather believe this is expressly the sort of deed that should be commemorated. In many cultures, the awarding of a medal recognizes this sort of deed.

When you start assembling the tin to cut up, keep in mind your idea for your medal and assemble the materials that will allow you to voice what you want to say in your amulet. Consider the implication of elements such as color, shape and overall form. Keep in mind that you're not making a picture, but assembling symbols.

Assemble your raw materials—tin cans, mint containers and old cookie tins are all good sources. You may want to cut out individual letters, whole words or entire insignias. Here, I started with the lid from a shoe-polish can. I prefer to use a saw, as I can get the finest detail. However, you may use tin snips or a combination of the two. Cut all the shapes and file the edges smooth.

CLEAN CUT

Tin is thin and will often bind while sawing (as will any thin material). To counteract this, place a couple of layers of cardboard beneath the tin and the problem is solved.

Look at your individual pieces of cut tin and decide their layout and where the rivets should go to secure the pieces to the background and to each other. Make a mark at those points. Remember that rivets reference attachment and strength, so you can use the rivets for the meaning they have as well as to hold the pieces together. Draw a line on the Faux Bone background where you want to cut out the shape. Here, I wanted to follow the contour of the tin, leaving a small amount of the background revealed.

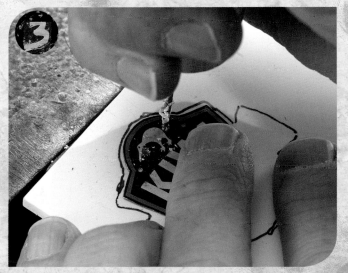

Using a #55 drill bit and working on scrap wood, drill the holes in the tin pieces.

Using the drilled tin pieces as a guide, drill one hole in one piece and insert a nail rivet to hold its place. It is very important to drill one hole only, or the pieces will not line up properly. Drill the next hole in the piece and insert the next rivet but only to hold its place; do not cut or hammer the nails down just yet.

Cut out the Faux Bone shape (see Faux Bone and Plexiglas, page 33) and sand it (see Sanding and Polishing, page 35). Apply color and any desired texture around the edges, such as that from a checkering file. Secure the tin to the Faux Bone with a couple nail rivets. To do this, begin by inserting wire nails through two of the center holes.

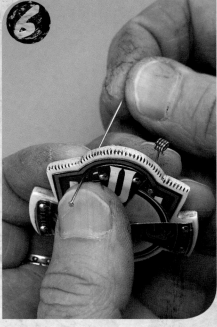

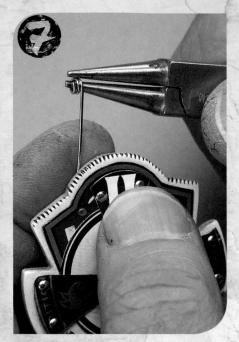

Turn the piece over and trim the nails so that about two playing-card's worth of wire is exposed from each. File the wires square and then set each with a round-faced hammer.

Continue setting the remaining rivets, one hole at a time. Drill two holes (#55) into the top of the piece for the hangers. Insert one 2" (5cm) headpin into one of the holes, from the front to the back.

Using round-nose pliers, begin at the end of the pin and create a coil (see Wire Coils, page 22) that will end about ½" (12mm) above the top of the piece.

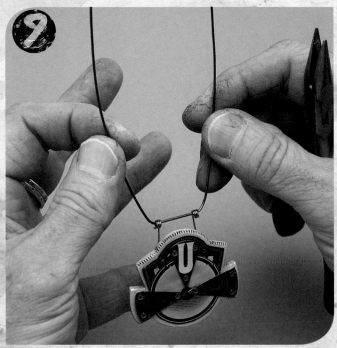

Repeat for the other headpin. Cut a 10" (25cm) piece of 19-gauge steel wire and thread it through both of the coils.

Where it passes through the coil, bend up each wire ninety degrees so the headpins fall straight down and the medal is level. (For the purposes of explanation, the left wire is wire "a" and the right wire "b.")

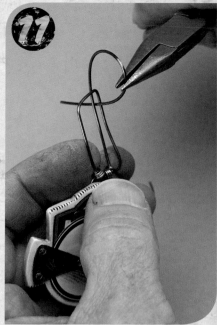

About ½" (12mm) above the coils, bend "a" over to cross "b" and vice versa. Wrap "a" around "b" at the bend in "b."

Repeat for wire "b" around "a."

Trim the right-hand wire down to about 2" (5cm). Coil it down to about ½" (12mm) above the bend on the right.

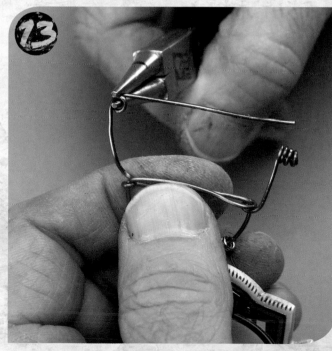

Trim the left-hand wire to about 2" (5cm). With the tip of the round-nose pliers, grasp the wire about ½" (12mm) above the coil and wrap the end of the wire around the round-nose pliers to form a spring (like the one on a safety pin).

Point the end of the wire (see Pointed Wire, page 24). Bend the wire horizontally so it can tuck into the opposite coil.

Finding Your Way

TOOLS

circle template

permanent marker

cross-peen hammer or similar

dead-blow or rawhide mallet

tin snips

bench pin

drill

$\frac{1}{16}$" (2mm) drill bit

metal wire brush

flat-faced hammer

wire cutters

bench block or similar

round-nose pliers

MATERIALS

24-gauge sheet metal

masking tape

small torch

19-gauge steel wire

micro-fasteners (nuts and bolts, size 0-80 or size 2-56)

ball compass (available at most grocery stores, auto stores or hardware stores as a dashboard accessory)

waxed linen cord

beads, pearls, any object with a hole large enough for the wire to slide through

cord or chain for hanging

The Vikings and other ancient cultures used a piece of magnetite or lodestone, hung by a cord, to help them locate magnetic north. This allowed them to navigate at sea in the event that their course was shrouded by fog. This amulet was designed to hang as a pendant around the neck and to act as a personal "lodestone." I made one for a friend and she has told me that when she feels a bit lost (figuratively speaking) she finds herself wrapping her hand around the pendant, closing her eyes and envisioning her way through. Does the amulet help? You can make your own and see for yourself.

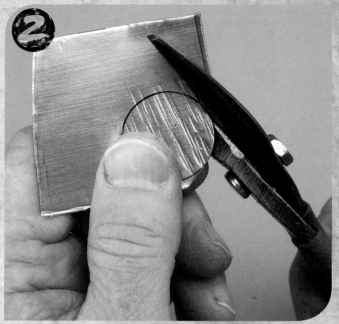

Using a circle template and a permanent marker, draw two 1" (3cm) circles on your piece of 24-gauge sheet metal. Before you cut them out, texture the circles with the cross-peen hammer then flatten the sheet with the mallet.

Using tin snips or the jeweler's saw, cut out the discs and reflatten with the mallet if needed.

A GOOD GRASP

When texturing metal with a hammer, hold the metal with your hands off the anvil to avoid hitting your hands with the hammer.

Tape the disks together. Using a circle template, center a ³⁄₈" (10mm) circle in the middle of the stacked discs and mark three holes in an equilateral triangle on the circle. Using a ¹⁄₁₆" (2mm) drill bit, drill the holes.

Mark the disks so you will be able to line up the drilled holes later. Patina the disks using the heat method (see Heat, page 44). Brush the disks using a metal wire brush until you get the finish you desire. Cut and clean three 10" (25cm) pieces of 19-gauge steel wire. Bend the wires into a V shape. Using micro-nuts and bolts, connect the two disks, but do not screw the nuts in all the way. Thread the V wires on the bolt shafts between the disks and tighten the nuts to secure the wires.

Cut the excess bolt shafts and rivet them (see Rivets, page 26).

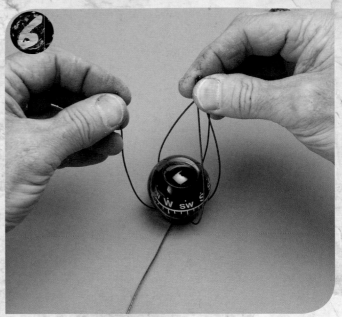

Set the compass on top of the metal disk and bend the wires up from the disk, bring them together at the top.

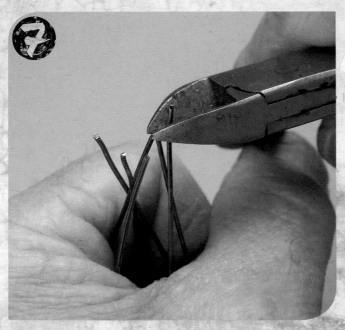

Trim the ends of the wires to make them even.

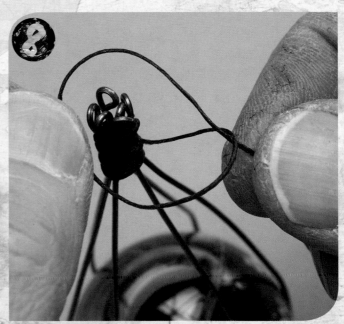

Make an outward-facing loop at the end of each wire. Cut a 16" (41cm) piece of red waxed-linen cord. Tie the end of the cord to one of the wires. Wrap the cord around the outside of the wires to secure the bundle together. With about 6" (15cm) of cord remaining, tie two half-hitch knots.

Trim the excess cord.

Rub your fingers over the waxed linen while spinning the compass cage to burnish the wax and help seal the thread. Cut seven pieces of any wire, which will fit through your beads ¾" (19mm) longer than the bead length. Using a flat-faced hammer, flatten one end of each wire.

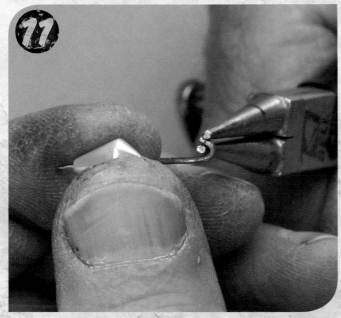

Thread one bead on each wire and create an eye at the top of each dangle.

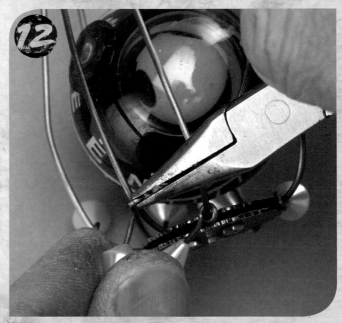

Attach six of the dangles to the base of the wires below the compass.

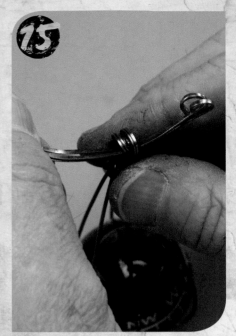

Cut one 4" (10cm) piece of 19-gauge steel wire. Using a flat-faced hammer, flatten the wire and then create an eye at one end. Attach the last bead dangle to the 4" (10cm) piece of wire. Thread the wire and bead dangle through the center of the gathered wires.

Using round-nose pliers, coil the excess flattened wire to create a bail.

Cut three 4" (10cm) pieces of 19-gauge steel wire and make a loop at one end of each wire. Hold the wires and create a slight curve. Thread the wires through the bail and loop the opposite ends.

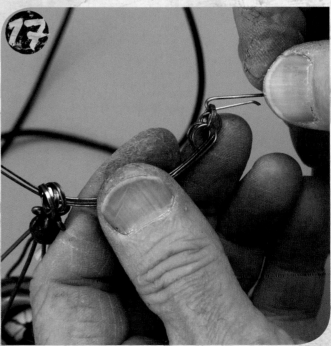

Create two jump rings from flattened 19-gauge steel wire (see Jump Rings, page 23). Use one jump ring to secure the three loops on both sides.

Attach a chain or cord of your choice using the jump rings.

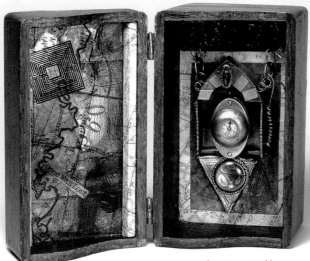

Photo: Evan J. Soldinger

ONCE WAS LOST
LINDA KAYE-MOSES

Neck piece—*sterling and fine silver, 14-karat gold, beetle elytra, quartz*
Nesting case—*found objects (copper, brass, oak), mica, transparency film, paper, gold foil*

BOLEYN BEAD
LISA CAIN

This is an amulet against beheading.
Silver precious-metal clay, sterling silver, garnet bullet cabs, pearls

ODIN'S COMPASS

The circle here is a reference to Odin, the Norse god, who pointed the way to Valhalla for Viking worriers.
Faux Bone, sterling silver, copper

SPLIT ROCK POWER OBJECT

TOOLS

medium file (wood files work well for the paper-pulp mâché)

wire scrap or palette knife

medium file

jeweler's saw

Faux Bone blade, fine

metal blade, #2/0

bench pin

silicon carbide (wet/dry) sandpaper, grits 300, 400, 600

wire cutters

flat-faced hammer

hammer or stamps for texturing the metal sheet

drill

⅛" (3mm) drill bit

small torch or liver of sulfur

two playing cards

flaring tool (eyelet setter)

bench block

round-nose pliers

MATERIALS

paper-pulp mâché

water

black acrylic paint

blue painter's tape

waxed paper

two-part epoxy resin

18-gauge wire

24-gauge sheet metal

⅛" (3mm) tubing

16-gauge wire

chain or cord for hanging

OPTIONAL

stationary belt sander

Rocks were, for perhaps thousands of years, the hardest substance in humankind's lexicon of materials. From rocks were made tools, weapons and protective barriers. If this were your relationship with rocks, what would you think if this hardest, most impenetrable substance was then cracked? What force is strong enough to commit such an act? Did this force crack the rock to reside in it? Is the force still there in that crack? Could the force be invoked or harnessed in some way? These are the sorts of questions I was thinking when I came up with the design for this next project.

Mix a batch of paper-pulp mâché with black acrylic paint (see Paper-Pulp Mâché, page 39). Form it into a patty, and crack, but do not separate, into three pieces. Set aside to cure.

Once cured, file the front and back of the paper-pulp mâché piece using a medium coarse file. Alternately, a belt sander can be used.

Place the paper-pulp mâché piece on blue painter's tape, then form a wall of tape around it. Place the pendant and tape on a level surface.

PRACTICAL AND PORTABLE

I use a 1" × 30" (3cm × 76cm) stationary belt sander (Harbor Freight) and find it wonderful for this and many other applications. It is inexpensive and light enough to be considered portable.

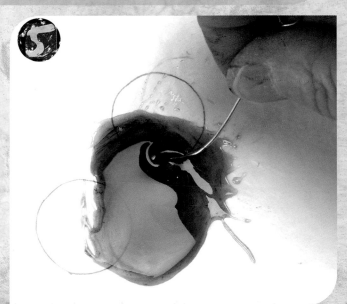

On a piece of white paper, trace a coin twice, leaving about ½" (12mm) between the two circles. Place a piece of waxed paper on top of the circles and squeeze a small amount of black acrylic paint in one corner. Squeeze a small amount of the resin—part "A"—into one circle and repeat for part "B" in the other (you can use the circles as a guide, but you need not fill the circles). Mix into one of the circles of resin, only about as much paint as would stick to the head of a pin.

With a scrap of wire or palette knife, mix the resin/paint thoroughly, adding similarly small amounts of paint until you can no longer see the drawn circle below. (Adding too much paint will interfere with the reaction of the resin, and it will never harden.) Join the two globs of resin and continue to mix until an even mixture is achieved.

Spoon the mixture into the cracks of the paper-pulp mâché. The resin should completely fill the cracks and slightly overflow. Set it aside to cure.

Remove the tape, and with a medium file, file the excess resin from the surface to reveal only the resin in the cracks. Cut to the desired shape with the jeweler's saw (and a Faux Bone blade) and file the sides to make the paper-pulp mâché form appear like rock. Without water, sand and polish the pendant, beginning with the 320-grit sandpaper, followed by the 400 and 600. Then turn the 600 over to the paper side and rub briskly.

Cut about a 4" (10cm) length of 18-gauge wire and file both ends to a point. Bend into a circle and hammer the wire with a metal hammer on a metal surface to harden it.

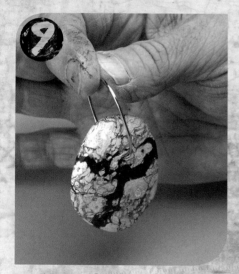

Use the pointed wire ends to grasp and balance the pendant. Adjust the wire's tension and move it around the pendant to determine the best spot to have it hang. Use a pen to mark the spot at the center of the gathered wires.

Using a ⅛" (3mm) drill bit, drill a hole through the pendant at the point you marked.

To make washers, draw two elliptical shapes on a piece of 24-gauge metal. If desired, texture the metal. Drill a ⅛" (3mm) hole in the center of each shape. Using the jeweler's saw, cut out the two washers.

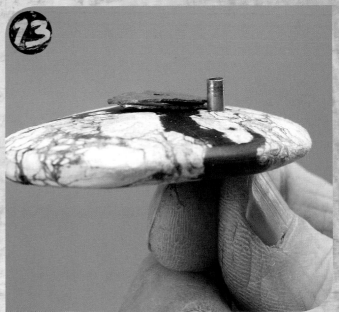

Patina the shapes using the heat method or liver of sulfur (see Patinas, page 44).

To measure the $\frac{1}{8}$" (3mm) tubing, insert it into the hole in the paper-pulp mâché piece and add on the thickness of the two washers plus about $\frac{1}{8}$" (3mm). Cut the tubing with the jeweler's saw, making sure the end is square. (A bit of filing may be done to ensure squareness.)

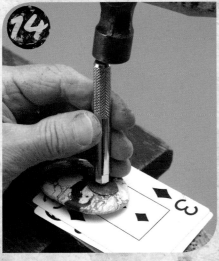

With the tubing in the paper-pulp mâché, slide a washer onto each side so there is $\frac{1}{16}$" (2mm) of tubing protruding from each washer. Place two playing cards, with a hole through them, on a metal block and place one end of the tubing through the hole so it rests on the metal block. With the eyelet/rivet flaring tool, tap the tubing on one end until the tubing starts to flare over. Repeat for the other end of the tubing and alternate between the two ends until the tubing is flared all the way over. You can tap the flared flanges with a hammer or leave them as is.

Cut a 4" (10cm) length of 16-gauge wire and hammer flat. At one end, form a spiral using round-nose pliers, and bend the wire ninety degrees at the base of the spiral. Patina the wire using the heat method or liver of sulfur. Insert the wire through the tubing with the spiral in front, and bend the wire up in the back of the pendant.

Coil the end of the wire to create a bale. Thread the pendant onto 30" (76cm) of ball chain, or chain of your choice.

U and Eye

TOOLS

ball-peen or round-faced hammer
wooden block
drill or pin vise
¹⁄₁₆" (2mm) drill bit
cross-peen hammer
bench block
torch or liver of sulfur
round-nose pliers
wire cutters
flat-faced hammer
vise
tweezers
polymer clay
medium file
side cutters
palette knife (preferably metal)
wax paper
toothpicks
scissors

MATERIALS

bottle cap
22-gauge metal strip ¼" × 3"
(6mm × 8cm)
#80 nuts and bolts
ephemera of any sort
PVA or craft glue
epoxy resin, 20-minute setting type
burnt umber acrylic paint
micro-washers and small beads
16-gauge wire

This amulet combines two of the most powerful and traditional amulet symbols in history: the horseshoe and the eye. The horseshoe is known in most cultures as something that offers protection for home and body by forming a container for good luck. That's why it's hung with the points up, like the letter U. The eye is worn on the body to stare down malevolent spirits and is one of the six ways to ward off evil. The bottle-cap "eye" allows you to include any symbol or image to be protected and the beads across the abstracted U act as amplifiers of the protective force of the amulet.

Using a ball-peen or round-faced hammer, create a round indent in a block of wood—preferably in the end grain (rough-cut side) of the block.

Using a ball-peen or round-faced hammer and working on the inside of the cap, hammer the ridges of a bottle cap into the indent in the wood to flatten the ridges out a bit, while keeping the dome shape of the cap. You have just created a bezel.

Using a ¹⁄₁₆" (2mm) (#52) drill bit, drill two holes one-third of the way down the bottle cap.

Draw a line down the center of the length of the metal strip. Place the strip on the edge of the bench block—right-handed people will work on the right side of the block; left-handed on the left. Beginning at the middle of the strip, position the cross-peen hammer with the cross-peen face perpendicular to the strip and tilt it slightly (just a few degrees) to the right or left accordingly. Begin hammering the strip, moving each hammer blow toward you. This will cause the strip to curve away from the edge and toward the center of the block. Hammer to the end closest to you, twisting the strip so you are always hammering perpendicular to the edge of the block.

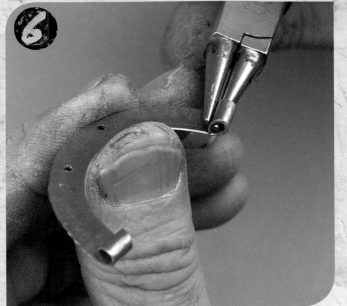

Holding the now curved part of the strip, hammer the other end of the strip to form a U about 2" (10cm) wide.

Paint the inside of the bottle cap if desired. I used red, but any color or pattern is fine. Position the bottle cap so the holes are over the strip and centered across its width. Drill one of the holes in the strip with the 1/16" (2mm) drill bit, insert a bolt to hold the place and drill the other hole.

File the ends of the metal strip. Patina the strip using either the heat method or liver of sulfur. Using round-nose pliers, curl the ends of the strip around once.

Mount the bottle cap to the metal strip using micro-nuts and bolts. The nuts are positioned on the back of the piece. Trim the bolts using wire cutters.

Secure any flat-faced hammer in a vise with the flat face up. Place the bottle cap facedown on the hammer so the bolt heads are on the face of the hammer. Use a hammer to rivet the bolt ends over the nuts (see Rivets, page 26).

Use ephemera of your choosing to create a collage in the bottle cap. Adhere the collage to the inside center of the bottle cap using PVA or craft glue.

Push the bottle cap assembly onto a piece of polymer clay to level and secure it. Mix some of the epoxy according to manufacturer's directions and drip some into the cap to cover the ephemera.

Once cured, you can add more layers of paper or draw with markers or similar and then add epoxy to fill to the top. Allow the epoxy to cure completely.

Cut a 4" (10cm) length of wire and hammer about 1" (3cm) of it flat on one end. Coil it around a pair of round-nose pliers a couple times and then insert the other end through one half of the U-shape. Begin threading on micro-washers and small beads, alternating between the two.

Continue alternating the beads and washers until the length of wire between the ends of the U is filled. Push the wire through the other end of the U and coil like the first. Mix a small batch of resin and add a pinprick amount of burnt umber acrylic paint to give it a sepia tone. Spread a thin layer of the tinted resin over the surface and add a bead, stone or other inclusion if desired. Set aside to cure thoroughly. Create coil clasps from 18-gauge wire (see Hook and Latch Clasp, page 25) and secure them to the ends of a cord and then to the ends of the coils on either end of the U-shape of the pendant.

THE POWER IS SAFE IN THE VOID

TOOLS

silicon carbide
(wet/dry) sandpaper

circle template

cross-peen hammer

center punch

drill or pin vise

#55 drill bit

1/16" (2mm) drill bit

wire cutters

jeweler's saw

metal blade, #2/0

bench pin

medium file

round-faced hammer

dapping block or wood block

tweezers

MATERIALS

baby food jar lid

permanent marker

19-gauge steel wire

24-gauge sheet metal

micro-bolt and nut

concrete mix and water

assorted beads

rubber or leather
cord and clasp findings

A rock with a hole in it is thought to have been the first prehistoric amulet. The belief may have been that the hole was made by a power greater than the rock itself—and certainly greater than any human. This was how the concept of a bead began. If one bead held this great power, many beads together must contain that power multiplied. In this amulet I have taken the beads off the strand and placed them in concrete to keep them safe and strong and to expose the hole so the power can be a visible thing. On the back, I placed a compass form to help direct that power.

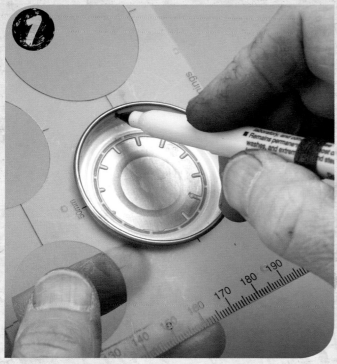

Sand off the desired amount of paint from a baby-food jar lid. Mark the quadrants of the lid using a circle template and a permanent marker.

Using a cross-peen hammer, texture the edge of the lid.

At the quadrants, using a #55 drill bit, drill a hole at the inside bottom of the lid where it meets the side of the lid.

At the quadrants, on the outside of the lid, use a center punch to make a small indent just under the lip of the lid. Again, using the #55 bit, drill holes at the four indents.

Cut four 2" (5cm) pieces of 19-gauge steel wire and bend them in half over a pencil. Working from the outside of the lid, take a bent wire and insert one leg into the top hole and one leg into the bottom hole at each quadrant. Push the legs into the cap until there is a 1/8" (3mm) loop left on the outside and bend the legs in opposite directions on the inside of the lid.

Using a 1/16" (2mm) drill bit, drill a hole in the center of the lid. Using a circle template, draw a circle on the sheet metal that is just a bit smaller than the top of the lid. Mark four quadrants and, on the outside of the circle, draw a small triangle pointing outward at each.

Using a 1/16" (2mm) drill bit, drill a hole in the center of the disk where the quadrants meet. Using a jeweler's saw, cut out the disc with points, and file and sand the flat surfaces and the edges. With a round-faced hammer, hammer the disc from the inside in a dapping block or in an indentation on the end grain of a wooden block (see page 105), to dome it slightly.

Patina the disk in liver of sulfur (see Liver of Sulfur, page 45). Finish the disk as desired, using a burnishing tool, steel wool or other methods. Secure the disk to the outside of the lid using a micro-bolt and nut. Trim off the excess bolt shaft.

9

Orient the points of the metal disk to center them between the wire loops, as they may have shifted when tightening the bolt.

THICKER THAN WATER

Mixing concrete a little thicker than recommended keeps the beads from sinking.

10

Level the lid on a piece of clay. Mix the concrete according to the manufacturer's directions. Fill the lid with concrete (see Concrete, page 38). Tamp the lid to get rid of any air bubbles. Using tweezers, place various beads into the concrete. Begin by placing large beads and then filling in with the smaller ones.

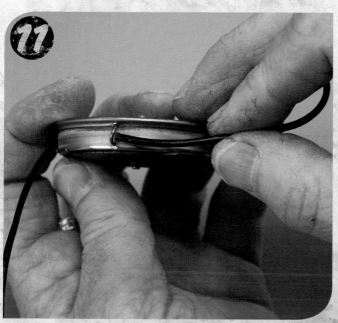

11

Allow the concrete to cure. Cut a length of cord to the desired size and string it through the wire loops around the piece.

12

Create a hook closure of your choice and secure it to the cord ends to finish.

MAGNIFYING YOUR PATH

TOOLS

wire cutters

tin snips

medium file

drill

#55 drill bit

1/16" (2mm) drill bit

bench pin

round-faced hammer

vise

dead-blow or raw-hide mallet

permanent marker

sandpaper, 600-grit

round-nose pliers

chain-nose pliers

circle template

craft knife

triangular scraper

1/8" (3mm) tubing

flat-faced hammer

MATERIALS

small magnifying glass lens

thin wire

baby-food jar lid

24-gauge sheet metal

nail, to fit snugly in a 1/16" (2mm) hole

micro-fastener nuts and bolts size 0-80 × 1" (3cm) long

cap nut

translucent and black polymer clay, 1/4 block each (conditioned)

19-gauge steel wire

OPTIONAL

patina materials

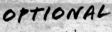

Sea captains often carried a spyglass to view the sea around them. They also carried a compass with a magnifying glass to help them view the charts that kept them on their appointed course. These were considered not just essential for navigation but good luck, as the captains often carried symbols of their home port on the back of these items. The compass surrounding the magnifying glass in this amulet has no orientation—only arrows marking four quadrants. There is no right or wrong direction to take, but there is the magnifying glass to help you see your options through a different lens. Perhaps you have a symbol of your home port to put on the back of yours.

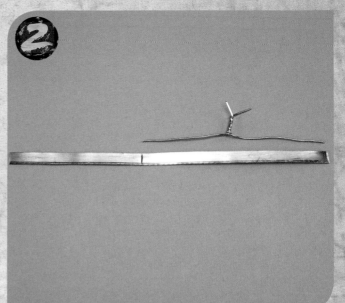

Cut 6" (15cm) of thin wire and form it into a circle, just slightly smaller than the size of the lens, twisting the ends together.

Use wire cutters to snip the wire loop someplace in the center and straighten the two sides. Using tin snips, cut a metal strip the same width as the inside height of the baby-food lid. Use the split wire to measure the length of the metal strip and then add ⅜" (10mm) to the mark.

Cut the metal strip at the mark and file the ends. Using a #55 drill bit, drill one hole at one end, measuring ⅛" (3mm) from the end.

Create a circle with the strip, overlapping the ends; the shape of the strip does not need to be a perfect circle. Using the #55 drill bit and the first hole as a guide, drill a hole into the other end of the strip.

Secure a round-faced hammer into a vise. Insert a nail from the inside of the circle to the outside and create a rivet (see Rivets, page 26), working on the head of the hammer.

Using a dead-blow hammer or raw-hide mallet, reshape the metal strip into a circle as needed.

Center the circle on top of the baby-food jar lid and, using a permanent marker, trace around the inside of the circle.

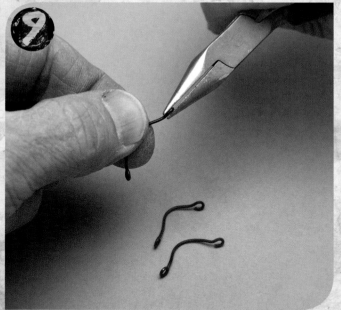

Sand the paint off the lid using 600-grit sandpaper.

Saw out the hole in the jar lid (see Piercing a Window, page 32). Cut three 1½" (4cm) pieces of 19-gauge iron wire. Using the smallest part of the round-nose pliers, create loops at both ends of each piece of iron wire. Bend each piece of wire over your index finger. Using chain-nose pliers, bend both loops of each wire to create brackets.

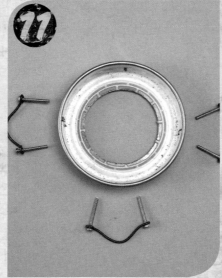

Place the lid into a circle template and mark the quadrants with a permanent marker.

Position the brackets around the lid with two on the sides and one at the bottom. The bolts will go through the brackets and into the side of the lid.

Hold each bracket at its position on the lid and mark the center of each bracket's loop. Using a $1/16"$ (2mm) drill bit, drill holes into the marks. Attach the brackets with nuts and bolts, with nuts on the inside of the lid.

Using round- or chain-nose pliers, bend the shafts of the bolts to the side and so they don't interfere with the window—either direction will work.

Using a $1/16"$ (2mm) drill bit, drill a hole in the top of a cap nut (drilling from the inside is easiest) and also on the side of the lid at the last marked quadrant (this will be the top of the pendant). Thread the microbolt throught the cap nut from the outside of the lid, to the inside and secure it with a nut on the inside in the same manner as the brackets. Bend the excess shaft of the bolt to the side.

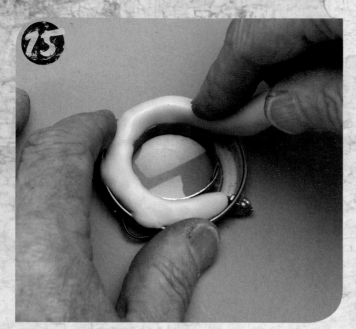

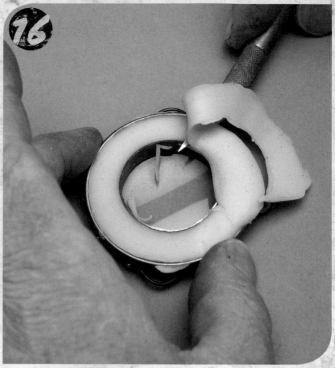

If desired, patina the copper ring using the heat method or liver of sulfur (see Patinas, page 44). Roll the polymer clay into a coil about ½" (12mm) in diameter and long enough to go around the inside of the lid. Press down on the side to make the coil flat on two sides in order to make it easier to slip into place. Place the lens inside the lid. Place the copper ring on top of the lens and center both in the lid. With the flat sides vertical, place the polymer clay coil into the space between the ring and the lid wall. Make sure the clay is pressed in firmly and evenly all around.

Using a craft knife, level the clay with the top of the lid and inner, metal ring.

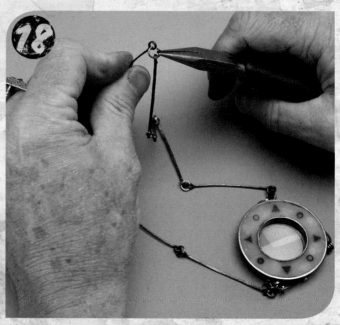

Press the tip of the triangular scraper into the clay in line with the brackets. Use ⅛" (3mm) tubing to make four circular indents in the clay. Bake according to package directions.

Finish the inlaying process with black clay (see Inlaying, page 37). Cut about a 30" (76cm) piece of 19-gauge steel wire. Using a flat-faced hammer, flatten the wire. Cut the flattened length into ten 2½" (6cm) pieces and file the ends of each piece square. Form a loop at the ends of each piece. Create ten to twelve jump rings from additional wire (see Jump Rings, page 23). Place three jump rings on each bracket. Connect each wire link using a jump ring, and connect the chain to the side brackets.

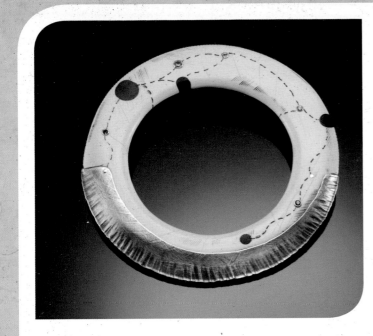

CELESTIAL CARTOGRAPHY BRACELET

We all need help from time to time while navigating our way through life. This bracelet has paths to follow, markers to check in with along the way and even pitfalls to avoid on the journey.

Faux Bone, sterling silver, epoxy resin, yellow topaz, citrine, ruby

NAVIGATIONAL AID #67

This piece was made for a woman beginning a new life for herself. The patterned silver in the center is a map, and it is mounted on a piece of iron—symbolically the metal of protection. The carnelian is for keeping a sense of humor as she faces the many changes ahead, symbolized by the small circles on the path surrounding the piece.

Sterling silver, rusted enameled iron, carnelian

SPIRIT BOAT PENDANT & EARRINGS

PAT GUILLETTE

Fine silver, sterling silver, gold-filled wire, amethyst, peridot, glass seed beads, forged and stamped sterling neck ring

Photo: Douglas Foulke

NEVER FAR

TOOLS

tin snips or jeweler's saw and #1 blade

vise

dead-blow or raw-hide mallet

medium file

cross-peen hammer

torch

flat-nose pliers

metal block

drill

¹⁄₁₆" (2mm) drill bit

bench pin or wood scrap for drilling

dull knife or stiff scrap of metal

round-nose pliers

brass brush

scouring pad (like Scotch-Brite)

burnisher

MATERIALS

22- or 24-gauge copper sheet, 3" × 1½" (8cm × 4cm)

19-gauge steel wire, 9" (23cm)

pearl, bead or other inclusion of your choosing

chain or cord for hanging

The pod form in this amulet has but one seed within its walls. The pod surrounds the seed but exposes the seed to the outside world. The seed can swing out from the pod, yet it remains attached and will always find its way back to the security of the pod.

I have made several of these amulets for friends who have children who are going off to college or to war. My friends give the pods to their offspring to let them know that they, as parents, are always there. Often, the parents want one for themselves to help them remember the same thing.

Using tin snips or a jeweler's saw, cut a piece of 24-gauge copper sheet 1" × 2¾" (3cm × 7cm). Draw a line down the center lengthwise. Set the piece in a vise and fold it along the line using a mallet.

After it is folded over ninety degrees in the vise, remove it and hammer it the rest of the way flat.

The edge with the fold is called the fold edge, and the open side is called the leg edge or leg side.

Draw in the boat shape, with the bottom of the boat on the leg (edge) side.

Cut the shape out with a saw or snips. File the edges. Put the piece in a vise and use a cross-peen hammer to upset the curved edge. You will need to reposition the metal in the vise a few times to get the whole thing.

Use a torch to anneal the piece. To do this, heat it while holding with a pair of pliers (or place on a heatproof surface). The piece should be heated until it just begins to show a dull orange color (it helps to see this if you darken the room a bit).

Place the piece on the metal block to heat-sink cool it or to let it cool on its own. Don't quench it in water, or the water will squirt all over when you begin the forging. Draw a slightly curved line from end to end halfway between the flat and curved edges. This line will be your guide as you begin forging your boat. To begin forging the boat see Forge Ahead, page 121.

Continue forging the piece along the fold edge until the fold edge is curved and the leg edge is straight.

Using a ¹⁄₁₆" (2mm) drill bit, drill a hole located on the guideline and ½" (13mm) down from one end.

Anneal the piece again and quench in water. Use a dull knife to pry the piece open.

When opened, you may want to pinch the sides with flat-nose pliers to make them straight or wiggle the edges with round-nose pliers. After shaping, brush with a brass brush and patina with heat or liver of sulfur and brush again. Clean the length of 19-gauge wire with a Scotch-Brite pad or steel wool and cut one 3" (8cm) and one 1½" (4cm) piece. File the ends. Thread the pearl onto the shorter wire (the pearl may need to be redrilled) and hammer one end flat to keep the pearl from sliding off. You can upset (texture) the short wire to match the edge of the boat by pinching it along its length with the round-nose pliers.

FORGE AHEAD

NOTE: *Right-handed people should work off of the right side of the block, and left-handed people, off of the left. My description will be for someone working right-handed.*

Using a cross-peen hammer, you will forge the fold edge of the metal. Position the boat with the fold edge lined up with the edge of the block. Hold the hammer with the face perpendicular to the edge of the block and your arm and the hammer handle in line with the edge of the block. IMPORTANT: Before you begin hammering, tilt your head just a little to the right. Observe how your arm, hand and ultimately the hammer tilt slightly. This is important, as it enables you to strike the metal more on the fold and less on the flat portion. It also allows you to keep the hammer blows on the right side of the line you drew. Both of these are important and, in fact, are what will cause the metal to bend in the final curve of the boat form.

With your fingers at the end of the metal farthest away from you, press the metal against the block. Beginning in the center of the fold edge, make a series of hammer blows on the fold edge, moving each blow toward you as you proceed. As you approach the pointed end, lighten your blows—you have much less metal to "move." (As you forge with the cross-peen hammer, check the shape of the indentations the hammer makes in the metal. Each indentation should be deeper and wider at the fold edge, tapering to a point at the halfway line you drew.) You will see the metal beginning to bend away from the hammer blows and curve to the left. It's important to keep turning the piece so the edge of the metal is on the edge of the block. When this half is hammered, hold the metal by the hammered end and, while still aligning it with the edge of the block, hammer the remaining half by moving the hammer blows away from you. Hold the already hammered portion of the boat off the end of the block so your hand is out of the way of the hammer as you finish forging.

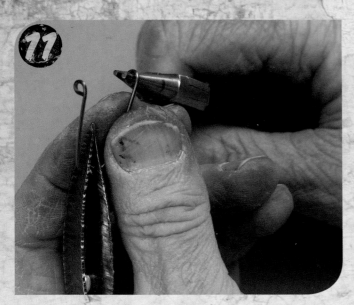

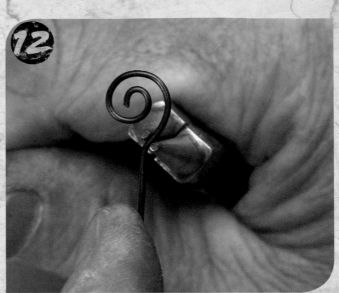

Create an eye on the other end of the pearl wire. Thread the 3" (8cm) length of wire through one hole in the side of the boat, then through the eye in the pearl wire (place the seam of the eye toward the back), then out through the other side of the boat. With the wire centered, bend it up in a gentle curve creating a U and form an eye at each end of the wire.

Hold the U by the eyes and swing the boat to make sure it moves freely. If it doesn't, widen the U a bit. Cut a length of chain (whose links will allow 19-gauge wire to pass through them) to a desired length. Cut a piece of 19-gauge wire 2½" (6cm) long and, using round-nose pliers, form an open spiral at one end.

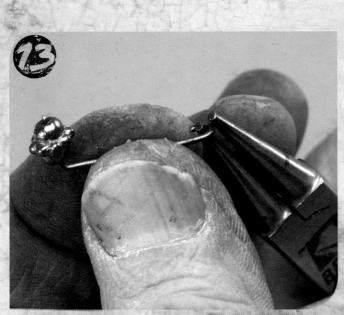

Make an eye loop at the other end. Cut another length of 19-gauge iron wire about 1¼" (3cm) long and hammer about ⅛" (3mm) of one end flat. File and sand the flattened end so it is smooth to the touch. Thread a bead onto the wire and up to the flattened end. Grasp the wire with the tip of the round-nose pliers just beneath the bead and bend the wire ninety degrees to form an L. Form the same size small eye as the spiral piece at the other end.

Attach the two clasp ends to the two ends of the chain. To close the clasp, thread the bead through the spiral.

JOURNEY COMPANION
DONNA PENOYER

As much as the creative process is a journey, for me it is a compelling and reassuring friend who urges me to go further on unknown paths. I cherish my dear fellow travelers with whom I play, and never feel alone when inventing my work. This whistle amulet empowers me to ward away doubt as I take steps in a new direction.
Metal clay

TRIANGLE BOX
CELIE FAGO
Fine silver, 24K gold, and brass (hinge pin)

TRANSPORT FOR A DREAM

Traditionally red coral is a good aid for meditation or visualization. The boat is symbolic of a journey. This piece is made to enhance the explorations of a person desiring or dreaming about pursuing a new path.
Sterling silver, epoxy resin, coral

CLOSURE FOR A MEMORY

TOOLS

scissors

jeweler's saw

metal blade, #2/0

bench pin

hammer

medium file

sandpaper

drill

⅛" (3mm) drill bit

#55 drill bit

burnisher

small torch

scouring pad (like Scotch-Brite)

brass brush

round-nose pliers

eyelet setting tool or small dapping punches

bench block

MATERIALS

photocopy of a person, place or object of significance

mica sheet

PVA glue

24-gauge sheet metal, two colors

scrap wood

rivet nail

⅛" (3mm) eyelets

bezel cup with matching cabochon stone

16-gauge wire

buttons

chain or cord for hanging

Amulets concerning our ancestors abound in virtually every culture. For centuries in western cultures, lockets have been a favorite form of jewelry with which to remember our ancestors. These amulets are usually a hinged compartment containing a picture, hair, teeth or other item belonging to the person to be remembered. The amulet of remembrance here is a takeoff on this idea. It includes an image of the person, a coin from his homeland and a carnelian at the top to represent his intellect. Hanging from the piece are buttons that acted as a closure for him on a shirt he used to wear and are now symbolic of buttoning up the memory of him in this amulet.

Begin with the portrait image you want to use. Tear it to the shape you desire. The image may be black and white or color—a photograph or copy manipulated on the computer or any combination thereof.

Spread PVA glue over the entire surface of the front of the image and adhere it to the mica.

Using scissors, cut around the image, leaving just a bit of space between the edge of the image and the cut edge of the mica.

Set the mica piece on a sheet of 24-gauge sheet metal and plan the background shape around the mica/image. Leave room for attaching an element to the top and also for setting the eyelets from which other elements will hang. I left some of the metal showing at the edges so I could texture it as part of the design. Cut the shape out using either tin snips or a jeweler's saw and a metal blade.

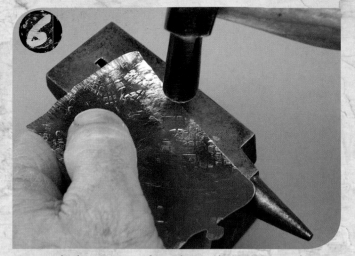

Decide on a shape that will go across the top of the piece. This shape will later have a stone set on it, and also be the element where the hanging mechanism will be attached. I decided on an umbrella shape that, for me, symbolizes the canopy that covers and protects a family. Cut the shape from a contrasting color of sheet metal (I used brass to contrast with the copper), and texture, file, sand and polish the piece. Set this piece atop the larger piece of metal and mark where the rivets will go to attach them together. Make another mark where the stone's bezel will later be set. Remove the top piece. On a piece of scrap wood, drill holes with the #55 drill bit at each of the marks. Set the piece back on the larger piece and drill the two holes for the rivets using the top piece as a guide.

Texture the larger piece of metal using hammers, punches or any other material to impart marks. On the back of the piece, I hammered a piece of metal screen against the copper to make the gridlike marks.

Patina the metal. Set the mica piece back on the front and decide where you would like to set a couple eyelets to secure the mica to the metal. Drill holes at those spots on the mica using a 1/8" (3mm) drill bit. Then, set the mica back on the metal, hold in place and drill one of the holes in the metal. Drop an eyelet in the hole, but don't set it, because it's just there to hold the mica in place. Drill the second hole.

Remove the eyelet and set the mica piece aside. Decide where you would like any additional holes from which to hang dangles and drill 1/8" (3mm) holes at those spots. Turn the piece over to the back, and decide where you would like an element on the back—like the coin I'm using here to represent my ancestor's homeland. Drill a hole in the element and then at an appropriate spot on the metal sheet where it can be riveted. I wanted to use a nail rivet here, but I didn't want the rounded head of the nail to interfere with the mica piece on the front, so I needed to file it flat first.

Set the nail rivet on the back to secure the element to the metal sheet. Set the eyelets into the ⅛" (3mm) holes drilled earlier. I sometimes like to set some from one side and some from the other.

Using nail rivets, secure the crowning element to the main piece. The heads of these nails do not need to be filed first unless you want them to look that way.

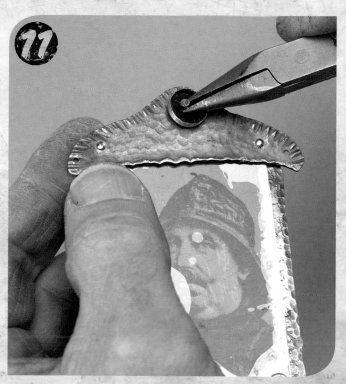

Drill a hole (#55) in the center of a small bezel cup. File the head of another nail. Insert the nail through the front of the bezel cup and then through the front of the crowning element.

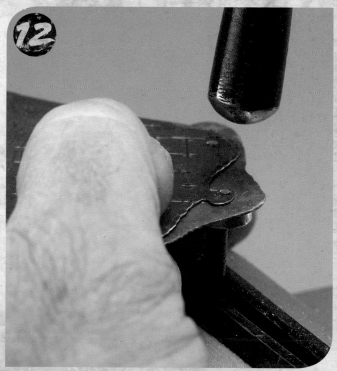

Trim the nail/rivet on the back and then form the rivet head by placing the bezel cup over a large nail head, or metal rod, that fits inside the cup. Hammer the end of the nail.

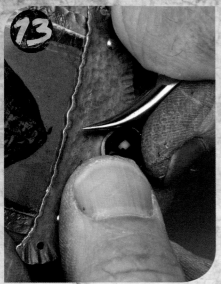

Set a cabochon in the bezel and then burnish the bezel over the stone using a burnishing tool.

Cut 2" (5cm) lengths of 16-gauge copper wire—one for each dangle and two more for the hangers. Ball one end of each wire by holding it vertically in front of the point of the blue cone of a flame of a butane torch. Heat about ⅛" (3mm) above the tip of the wire until the end turns bright orange, begins to sparkle and balls up.

Polish each wire a bit with a scouring pad and scrub with a brass brush. Thread a button onto a balled wire and then thread the nonballed end through an eyelet hole from the back to the front of the large copper piece. Form a spiral or other design with the end of the wire so it will not pull back through the eyelet hole and so the button will dangle from the bottom of the piece. Bend the wire so the design in front lies flat against the piece and so the button dangles freely. Repeat for each eyelet.

Thread the remaining balled wires through the holes on either side of the crowning element from the front to the back. Bend the wires up and then create a spiral on their tails.

Cut two more lengths of 16-gauge wire to 2" (5cm) and flatten with a hammer. Form a loop large enough to accommodate the spiral hangers, on each end with round-nose pliers. Twist open one loop and attach it through one of the spirals. Close the loop. Repeat for the other spiral. Attach the other end to a chain or cord.

PIN FOR MILAN

This is a very personal piece for me. The button is from a sport coat my father bought on one of his many trips to England when I was quite young. Upon his death, I didn't keep many of his belongings but did remove the buttons from jackets he wore as sort of charms of remembrance. Here, the button is the body of the piece, and the carnelian is at the top to protect his memory in my mind. The aquamarine in the center refers to his spirit and great peace he projected. I am the pearl at the bottom, not just hanging, but wrapped in his memory.

Sterling silver, leather button from an old jacket, pearl, aquamarine

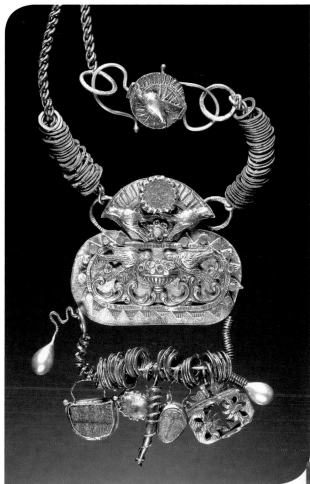

BIRDSONG

LINDA KAYE-MOSES

Sterling and fine silver, 18-karat gold, Montana sapphire, Febrile Glass (Tiffany Studios), cultured pearl, trilobite, found objects (leather, velvet, 24-karat gold foil, sterling silver, wood, brass), acrylic paint, mica

Photo: Evan J. Soldinger

LOOKING BACK BEAD

TOOLS

compass or circle template

jeweler's saw

Faux Bone blade, fine

bench pin

heat gun or toaster oven
(embossing heat gun is fine)

dapping die and punch
(see A Dapper Design, page 131)

silicon carbide sandpaper
grits 320, 400, 600

circle template

vise

scribe or similar

files

Dremel rotary tool or similar

hand drill or pin vise

#55 drill bit

round-nose pliers

MATERIALS

$\frac{1}{16}$" (2mm) Plexiglas, clear
and black, about a 2" (5cm)
square of each

masking tape

ephemera and items from your
past that can fit inside the bead

Plexiglas solvent or cyanoacrylate
glue (like Zap-A-Gap)

needle bottle applicator for the
solvent or a small thin brush

acrylic paint

paper towels

$\frac{1}{4}$" (6mm) Faux Bone

18-gauge wire, 5" (13cm)

cord or chain for hanging

Another nod to a traditional locket is this bead that encloses reminders from several different times in my life rather than just a single person or event. The items were chosen for their history. Then the items were combined with new materials that allowed me to introduce images and ideas from my present. Employing neutral materials like Faux Bone or Plexiglas allows me to imbue them with just the expression I want without having to deal with the references they bring with them.

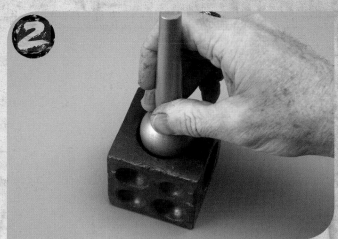

Cut a circle from the black Plexiglas with about a 1¼" (3cm) diameter. You need not file the edges at this time. Set the circle in a dapping block (see A Dapper Design, this page) and heat from above with a heat gun. Alternately the disc can be heated in a 265°F oven and removed after about two minutes.

When the plastic is softened, push the dap into the block to dome the plexi.

Let the plastic cool for a few seconds and then remove it from the block.

A DAPPER DESIGN

To form the circles of Plexiglas into half-bead shapes, you must heat the circles and push them into a concave hemisphere or "well," using the shape of a sphere to push. The sphere (or a half-sphere may be used) must have a diameter just a tad smaller than that of the well. The well is called a dapping die or dapping block, and the sphere is called a dapping punch or dap. You can buy sets of matching dies and daps (pictured here), or any container with a smooth, hemispheric interior will do for the block, and anything that will fit exactly inside that container will do for a dap. Some alternatives for dies are measuring cups, measuring spoons or soup ladles. Alternatives for daps include wadded-up paper towel, smaller spoons and wooden balls found in crafts shops. These wooden balls can also be pushed into conditioned polymer clay and baked, after which the ball is the dap and the clay is the die.

Form a tab with masking tape by taking a 1½" (4cm) piece of masking tape and folding it in half but allowing the ends to bend out at right angles away from the tape fold to form "wings." Push these wings against the top of the dome so the tape fold is now pointing up and you can hold on to it. Place a piece of 320-grit sandpaper on a smooth, even surface, and drip some water onto it. Holding the tape handle, place the dome on the wet sandpaper and rub it on the sandpaper in a figure-eight motion until the edges are sanded down so the edge of the dome is sharp and even. The flat "flange" should extend evenly from the inside to the outside of the half bead.

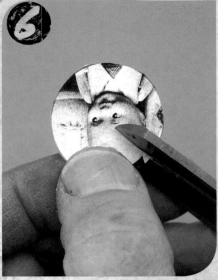

Repeat steps 1 through 4, this time using clear Plexiglas, to create a second dome of the same size. Using a circle template, draw around an image that will be the background of the inside of the bead.

Cut out the image and then cut from the outside of the image to the center of the circle.

Spread glue over the backside of the image and adhere to the inside of the black half bead. The slit in the paper will allow the paper to conform to the inside curve without buckling.

Set the tab of the black half bead in a vise to hold it. Place the objects for inclusion in the half bead and set the clear half on top, lining up the edges. Put some solvent in the squeeze bottle or dip a small brush into the solvent and deposit a drop of solvent at the edge. The solvent will wick around the two pieces by itself. Introduce more drops of solvent at various points along the edges as necessary to form a continuous seal. Note: When using the bottle, tilt it and a drop will come out; it's not necessary to squeeze.

When the bead has cured (about two hours), sand only the black Plexiglas with 600-grit sandpaper—don't sand the clear. When sanded, you can scratch a pattern or design into the back of the black plexi with a scribe, an awl or an electric engraver. Rub paint into the inscribed lines and rub off with a paper towel.

File the edges of the seam and then sand and polish.

On a piece of ¼" (6mm) Faux Bone, draw a shape that will become a holder for the plexi bead. With a rotary tool and a separating disc (or jeweler's saw and Faux Bone blade), slice through the thickness of the Faux Bone about ⅜" (10mm) from the outside, in.

Cut out the shape with the jeweler's saw and a Faux Bone blade and file and sand smooth (see Filing, Sanding and Polishing, page 34). With a heat gun, heat the section that has the cut.

When the Faux Bone is warm and pliable enough, spread out the two halves and push the plexi bead between them.

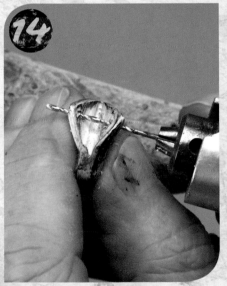

Let the Faux Bone piece cool, then texture/decorate/color the piece as desired. Drill a hole through both halves of the spread-apart portion using a #55 drill bit.

Set the bone piece back on the plexi bead and drill into the plexi at the spot of the holes, first from the front and then from the back. (Don't try to go all the way through the plexi bead and bone in one shot.)

Draw a ball on the end of a 5" (13cm) piece of 18-gauge wire. Insert the wire through the bone, then the plexi bead, then the bone, from the front to the back so the ball on the wire is in the front. Fold up the wire and then use round-nose pliers to make an irregular coil bale on the entire length of the wire. Thread whatever cord or chain you choose through the bale to finish.

SEEING THROUGH

We have all hit the proverbial "wall" at some time. It may have been when you were tired, over-loaded or sad. Maybe it was a math problem or a deficit in money—perhaps the inability to make a choice or institute a change. Whatever may have constructed that wall, getting around or over it can be difficult. This amulet is your chance to take a symbol of that change, problem or sadness, to make that wall and then to see your way right through. Here, the concrete is the wall, the glass your way into it, and the images behind the glass the situation that may now be dealt with clearly.

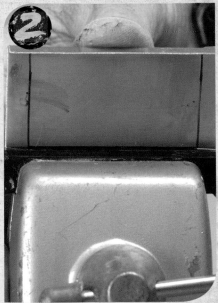

Draw a line along on each side of the copper sheet, ¼" (6mm) from the edge. Using the jeweler's saw, cut into the short sides of the metal along the lines, stopping at the first intersecting line.

Place the long side of the metal in the vise so you can just see the line above the top of the vise. Fold the sheet over the top of the vise to form a ninety-degree angle and hammer the fold gently. Repeat for the other side.

Using square-nose pliers, grasp one of the short edges just above the line and bend along that edge. File and sand the tabs that extend from the long side of the metal (see Filing, Sanding and Polishing, page 34).

Using the flat-nose pliers, fold the tabs over the outside of the short side and cinch the tab and side together. Repeat on the other side.

Using a center punch, make an indent on each tab at the corner. Using a #55 drill bit, drill a hole through each indent.

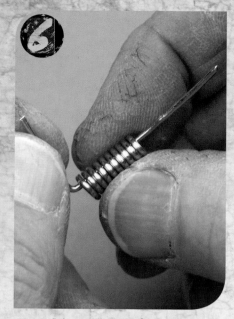

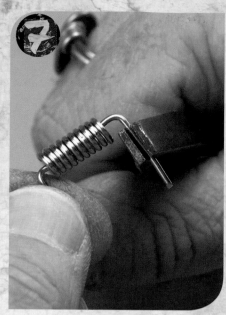

Cut a 4" (10cm) piece of 16-gauge wire that will become a staple to fit through the holes at one end of the box. Bend one leg of the staple at a 90-degree angle. Make a coil about ½" (12mm) long and thread it onto the staple.

Bend the other leg of the staple at a 90-degree angle as well.

Using square-nose pliers, insert the staple legs into the holes at one end of the box and cinch against the short side. This will become the top of the box.

Repeat steps 5 through 7, excluding the coil, for the other side. With one round-nose pliers prong in the center, grasp one side of the plain staple and bend up. Repeat with the other side, placing one prong in the same center spot.

Cut a 2" (5cm) piece of 16-gauge wire. Thread it through the coil at the top and bend up both sides.

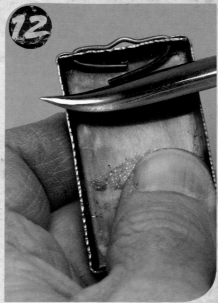

Using round-nose pliers, form two eyes on the ends of the wire, making sure the seam of the eye is toward the back of the piece.

Scour the outside of the box using a Scotch-Brite pad or steel wool. Texture the open edge of the box (see Surface Textures, page 41). Patina the box using liver of sulfur (see Patinas, page 44), and highlight the copper using the Scotch-Brite pad or steel wool. Use a burnisher to highlight the textured edges.

If desired, use a scribe to write/scratch a message on the inside of the box. It will later be covered with the concrete, but you (and anyone you choose to tell) will know it's there.

Age a section of photocopied text using a little bit of shoe polish on a cut-off bristle brush.

Place a piece of broken glass over the text and find some text you like. Put a thin layer of glue over the text, wiping most of it off with your finger. Put the glass on the wet glue and let it dry. Repeat steps 14 and 15 for other elements you would like to use, such as a map. When the paper is dry on the back, trim it around the edges of the glass, using a craft knife.

Mix concrete according to the manufacturer's directions. Fill the box with cement and tamp it to rid it of air bubbles. Use tweezers to imbed the pictures, glass and other any other object you want into the concrete.

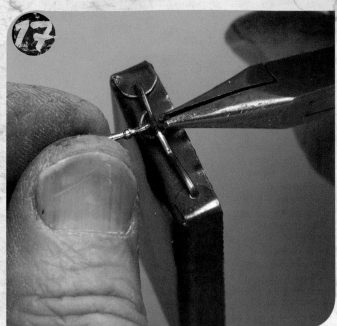

Let the cement set. Use a metal brush to remove the skin of the cement. Attach a dangle to the bottom of the box.

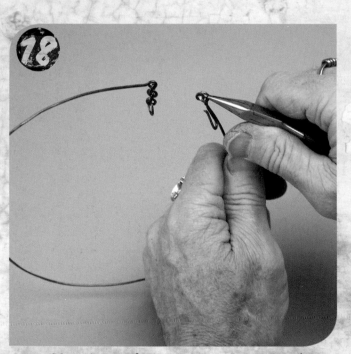

Cut a 16" (41cm) piece of 16-gauge copper wire. Texture the wire using an old flat-faced hammer and the side of the anvil, and bend the wire into a circle shape. Patina the wire using liver of sulfur. Make an eye at each end of the wire. Make three jump rings (see Jump Rings, page 23) and one hook. Secure the jump rings to one of the eyes and the hook to the other.

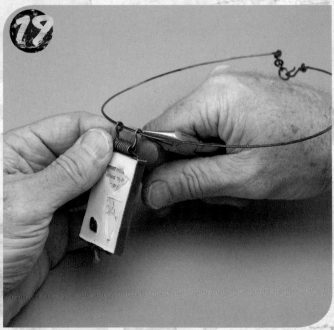

Open the eyes in the U shape at the top of the piece by twisting to one side. Hook on the circular wire and twist the eyes closed.

BRUNSWICK-BRACELET
MAGGIE BERGMAN

Relocating from a rainforest environment to the inner city left me feeling lost. Taking to the streets with my camera, focusing and familiarizing myself with the neighborhood's architectural detail and textures, helped me find a sense of place. Wearing this jewelry opened dialogue with people, furthering a spirit of community.
Metal clay, paper-based images, resin

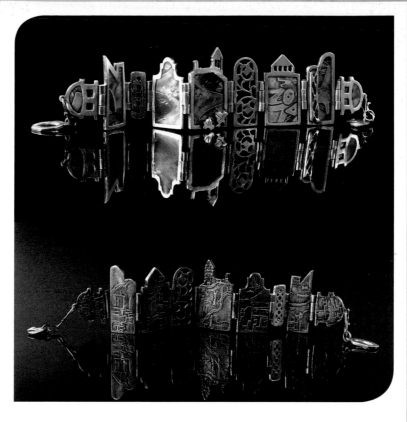

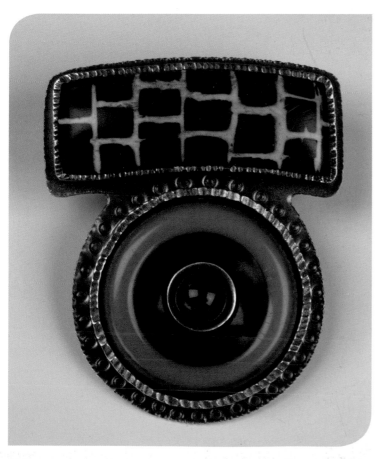

BRICK PIN

The bricks represent the wall one's mind can hit from time to time. The carnelian represents protection—there to guard against the wall that can have too much power.
Sterling silver, polymer clay, antique button, carnelian

139

RESOURCES

The suppliers listed here are all excellent resources for the tools and materials used in this book, but be sure to always check your local jewelry and hardware stores. I have included Web addresses where applicable, and I encourage you to go to their Web sites—if nothing else—to browse to see what you come up with. Just seeing a new tool or material may start you on your way to new work.

CLAY FACTORY INC.
polymer clay
www.clayfactoryinc.com

FIRE MOUNTAIN GEMS
jewelry supplies
www.firemountaingems.com

HARBOR FREIGHT TOOLS
general tools
www.harborfreight.com

MSC INDUSTRIAL SUPPLY CO.
tools, drill bits, power tools, tubing
www.mscdirect.com

POLYMER CLAY EXPRESS
polymer clay, jewelry findings and more
www.polymerclayexpress.com

PROGRESSTOOL MACHINE & TOOL CORP.
jewelry tools
www.progresstool.com

SMALL PARTS
tubing, threaded rod
www.smallparts.com

RIO GRANDE
jewelry supplies
www.riogrande.com

ROBERT'S REAL FAUX BONE
Faux Bone, saw blades, Plexiglas, checkering files, micro-bolts and nuts and more
www.fauxbone.com

SHERRI HAAB
transfer medium and more
www.sherrihaab.com

WHOLE LOTTA WHIMSY
WhimsyCrete (concrete mix) and more
www.wholelottawhimsy.com

NOW PAINT THE TOWN RED
ANGELA BAUSUEL-CRISPIN
From the Urban-Ethnic series
Metal clay, Faux Bone, sterling silver, silk bristles

INSPIRATION

The books listed here are some of those I have found, both inspiring and informational, about amulets, talismans and living on this planet with others.

Amulets of the Goddess: Oracle of Ancient Wisdom by Nancy Blair, 1993 Wingbow Press

Amulets: Sacred Charms of Power and Protection by Sheila Paine, 2004 Inner Traditions

Amulets and Talismans by Migene González-Wippler, 1991 Llewellyn Publications

Body Guards: Protective Amulets and Charms by Desmond Morris, 1999 Element Books

Egyptian Magic by E. A. Wallis Budge, 1971 Dover Publications

The Gift by Lewis Hyde, 1979 Vintage Books

Harold and the Purple Crayon by Crocket Johnson, 1955 HarperCollins

Talismans and Amulets by Felicitas H. Nelson, 2000 Sterling Publishing

The Tao of Pooh by Benjamin Hoff, 1982 Penguin Books

CONTRIBUTING ARTISTS

ANGELA BAUSUEL-CRISPIN
www.langeestla.com
www.angelacrispin.canalblog.com
ange.est.la@wanadoo.fr

MAGGIE BERGMAN
www.maggiebergman.com.au
info@maggiebergman.com.au

LISA CAIN
www.mcsj.co.uk
info@mcsj.co.uk

CELIE FAGO
www.celiefago.com

PAT GUILLETTE
www.howlingmoonstudio.com
www.howlingmoonstudio.blogspot.com
howlingmoonstudio@sbcglobal.net

JENNIFER KAHN
www.jenniferkahnjewelry.com

LINDA KAYE-MOSES
www.paradisecityarts.com/artpage/mixedmedia/lindakayemoses.html
evansol@berkshire.net

DONNA PENOYER
www.donnapenoyer.com
art@donnapenoyer.com

INDEX

ABOUT ROBERT

Robert Dancik has been an artist/teacher for a really long time now. He started with teaching little kids (5–10 years old) for about fifteen years, where he learned from them that play can be serious work and vice versa. He then taught high school for twenty years, where he learned that it does get more and more curious. He now teaches graduate school but spends most of his teaching time traveling about the world instructing workshops and meeting all sorts of fascinating folks.

His degrees are in fine art and sculpture but he's mostly interested in just making things. Sometimes the thing he makes is jewelry, sometimes sculpture, sometimes furniture and sometimes dinner.

He has artwork in a number of books and he writes for several magazines. He shows his artwork in museums and galleries in the United States and elsewhere, and he has work in both public and private collections.

Robert presently lives in Cornwall, England, where he collects drums, is an avid cook, and is surrounded daily by magic and beauty.

www.robertdancik.com
www.fauxbone.com
playcik@yahoo.com

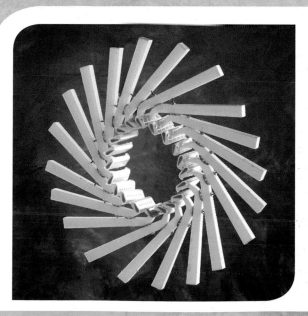

REALLLLLLY CLOSE
Bic razors, brass nuts, bolts and washers

INDULGE YOUR CREATIVE SIDE WITH THESE OTHER F+W MEDIA TITLES

A CHARMING EXCHANGE

KELLY SNELLING AND RUTH RAE

Inside *A Charming Exchage* you'll find the works and words of more than 30 artists with an array of varying creative styles and insights on collaborative art. Learn how to create 25 jewelry projects using a wide variety of techniques, from working with basic jewelry findings, beads and wire to incorporating mixed-media elements such as solder, fabric and found objects into charms and other jewelry projects. The book even offers ideas, inspiration and resources for you to start your own online swaps and collaborations.

ISBN-10: 1-60061-051-X
ISBN-13: 978-1-60061-051-6
paperback, 128 pages, Z1653

ALTERED CURIOSITIES

JANE ANN WYNN

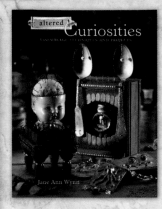

Discover a curious world of assemblage with projects that have a story to tell! As author Jane Wynn shares her unique approach to mixed-media art, you'll learn to alter, age and transform odd objects into novel new works of your own creation. Step-by-step instructions guide you in making delightfully different projects that go way beyond art for the wall—including jewelry, hair accessories, a keepsake box, a bird feeder and more—all accompanied by a story about the inspiration behind the project. Let *Altered Curiosities* inspire you to create a new world that's all your own.

ISBN-10: 1-58180-972-7
ISBN-13: 978-1-58180-972-5
paperback, 128 pages, Z0758

PLEXI CLASS

TONIA DAVENPORT

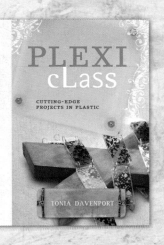

Discover a modern, industrial twist on mixed-media art jewelry. *Plexi Class* features 30 cutting-edge projects that all start with plastic such as Plexiglas, vinyl or shrink plastic. In addition to learning how to cut Plexiglas, you'll also learn how to shape it into earrings, charms and pendants, and you'll see how easy it is to combine plastic with your favorite papers, embellishments and other mixed-media materials.

ISBN-10: 1-60061-061-7
ISBN-13: 978-1-60061-061-5
paperback, 128 pages, Z1753

SEMIPRECIOUS SALVAGE

STEPHANIE LEE

Create clever and creative jewelry that tells a story of where it's been, as metal, wire and beads are joined with found objects, some familiar and some unexpected. You'll learn the ins and outs of cold connections, soldering, aging, using plaster, resins and more, all in the spirit of a traveling expedition.

ISBN-10: 1-60061-019-6
ISBN-13: 978-1-60061-019-6
paperback, 128 pages, Z1281

THESE BOOKS AND OTHER FINE NORTH LIGHT TITLES ARE AVAILABLE AT YOUR LOCAL CRAFT RETAILER, BOOKSTORE OR ONLINE SUPPLIER, OR VISIT US AT **WWW.MYCRAFTIVITY.COM**.